The
East–West Pendulum
Revisited

Robert Lloyd George

D0300686

2005

For my friends in Asia

China – there lies a sleeping giant.
Let him sleep, for when he wakes, he will shake the world ...
NAPOLEON

But nothing of the conflicts of British party politics counted much against
the great movements in history. None of our struggles mattered much, wars
or revolutions or what you will, as compared with the sheer biological and
geographical facts. Whatever happened, in two hundred years, perhaps
sooner, the balance of the world would have changed. The industrialization
of Russia was taking place: India would follow: perhaps China, within a
hundred years.

Whatever Governments presided over the operations, these changes would
make our local concerns look no more significant than the War of the Roses.
DAVID LLOYD GEORGE
Quoted by C. P. Snow, *Variety of Men*

Trade with the Far East was only possible thanks to exports
of gold and silver ...

So during the sixteenth and seventeenth centuries there circulated
throughout the vast Asian continent, source of spices, drugs and silk, the
precious gold and above all silver coins minted at Venice, Genoa or
Florence, and later the famous Spanish pieces of eight. Away to the East
flowed these currencies, out of the Mediterranean circuit into which it had
often required so much patience to introduce them. The Mediterranean as a
whole operated as a machine for accumulating precious metals, of which, be
it said, it could never have enough. It hoarded them only to lose them all to
India, China and the East Indies. The great discoveries may have
revolutionized routes and prices, but they did not alter this fundamental
situation, no doubt because it was still a major advantage to westerners to
have access to the precious merchandise of the East, in particular pepper,
which according to one Venetian 'brings with it all the other spices ...';
no doubt also because in the sixteenth century, as in the past, the
purchasing power of precious metals rose above that of Christian
countries as soon as one crossed the border into the Orient.
FERNAND BRAUDEL
The Mediterranean in the Age of Philip II

Oh East is East, and West is West, and never the Twain
Shall meet
Till Earth and Sky stand presently at God's great
judgement seat
But there is neither East nor West, Border nor Breed,
nor Birth
When two strong men stand face to face, though they
come from the Ends of the Earth.
RUDYARD KIPLING

The balance-sheet of cultural influences is overwhelmingly one-sided.
The world gave back to Europe occasional fashions, but no ideas or
institutions of comparable effect to those Europe gave to the world...
For centuries, thousands of European ships sailed to Calicut, Nagasaki and
Canton. During those same centuries, not one Indian, Japanese or
Chinese ship ever docked at Tilbury, Genoa or Amsterdam.
J. M. ROBERTS
A History of the World

Our earth is degenerate in these latter days; bribery and corruption
are common; children no longer obey their parents; every man wants to
write a book, and the end of the world is evidently approaching.
TRANSLATION FROM AN ASSYRIAN TABLET FROM 4000 BC

According to the eighteenth-century economist DAVID RICARDO, each time
a new country joins the table of world trade, everyone is enriched.

Contents

Charts, tables and maps

Acknowledgements

During the course of writing a new edition of *The East–West Pendulum*, I conducted a number of interviews in Asia; two of which, with Professor Edward Chen and T. L. Tsim, both in Hong Kong, were with old friends whom I had consulted for the first edition fifteen years ago. I would like to thank them, and also Abraham Lue, for their time and valuable insights.

I also had the privilege of meeting in Beijing with Ambassador Wu Jianmin, President of the Foreign Affairs School for Chinese diplomats, and US Ambassador Clark T. Randt, Jr. My old friend, Philip Snow, has once again corrected my Chinese nomenclature and history, and given me valuable guidance and help. It goes without saying that the views expressed in this book are my own, except where specifically stated otherwise and that I take full responsibility for the forecasts and opinions contained in the book. For instance, I have retained Marco Polo as 'the first Westerner to visit China' though this can never be conclusively proved: he may have had a vivid imagination, but he also knew a lot about Asia and its people.

My colleagues at Lloyd George Management in Hong Kong and in London have been very supportive and helpful, especially M. F. Tang, Christopher Tang and Amanda Whitmore Snow, May Ling Wee, Gautam Senghal, Samir Mehta and of course thanks to Kim Waterfield.

Preface

In ancient times Chinese people explained the nature of the world as a basic dualism. Yang is male, light, hot, active; yin is female, dark, cold, passive. Unlike the dualism of the Mediterranean world, in which good and evil are in perpetual conflict, yin and yang are mutually complementary and balancing. The greater yang grows, the sooner it will yield to yin; the sun at noon is starting to give way to night. The interdependence of the two principles is well symbolized by an interlocking figure which today is used as the central element in the flag of the Republic of Korea. Actually, the yin–yang concept often seems more useful than Western dualism for analysing nature and also human affairs. It neatly fits the rhythms of day and night, summer and winter, and the balancing roles of male and female.

This dualism may also be applied to East and West. The East has, for the past thousand years or more, had a great preponderance in terms of the numbers of humanity, of economic resources and of continuous civilization. Why did the Chinese Empire recover from the early barbarian incursions of the early fourth century when its contemporary in the West, the Roman Empire, collapsed and declined into the Dark Ages? On the other hand, the question may be asked, why did China never have an age of exploration and science such as the West's Renaissance, or the Age of Enlightenment? Despite Western supremacy in the field of ideas, it was only from 1800 onwards that Western traders and colonial powers managed to dominate the Asian peoples.

The argument of this book is that Asia is once again on the move. It has already replaced the United States as the locomotive of the world economy with its new spending power, its new technology and its growing capital resources. Within Asia the leadership is changing too. Japan led the wave of modernization after the Second World War. It led in management and technology and has maintained a stable political system. Now, however, it is China which is taking up the baton. My contention is that the leadership of Asia, in economic and cultural terms, is passing to the Chinese.

There are sound arguments for this prediction. The first is the proven genius of the Chinese race throughout the past 3,000 years of continuous civilization. The accomplishments of the Chinese people in the field of scientific and technological invention as described by Joseph Needham in his book *Science and Civilisation in China*, are a further proof of the creativity and artistic brilliance exhibited in Chinese paintings, ceramics and literature. For example, the great surviving monuments of the early Ming Dynasty, the Forbidden City and the Temple of Heaven in Peking, may be compared with the remarkable construction of the Chinese city states of Singapore and Hong Kong in the past thirty years. An age of large-scale building activity reflects the underlying confidence of the culture.

As we approach the year 2008, when the Olympic Games will be held in China for the first time in the 110 years of modern Olympic history, we shall see China visibly taking its place as a modern civilized country and as a great power in the world. Beijing, a city of nearly 20 million, will become the focus of this new age of confidence and construction. The new Olympic Village lies directly north of the Forbidden City, on the ancient north–south line prescribed by the Chinese geomancers over 1,000 years ago. Beijing is a world city, comparable with London, Paris, Berlin or Washington.

My purpose in writing this book is to analyse the risks and rewards for investors in Asia today. As in the first edition of the book, I have based much of this analysis on history and on the political risks which have consistently reappeared in Chinese history because they are our only guide to the unforeseeable future.

Since I wrote the first edition in 1991, much has changed in Asia, and it has changed especially rapidly in China. I believe, today, more than ever, that this is the region which is likely to impact the lives of our children over the next 50 or 100 years. It becomes every year more vitally important to understand Chinese history, language and culture, the roots of the Chinese family and the family business and of China's relationships with other peoples and countries.

1

Introduction

> The best prophet of the Future is the Past
> BYRON

He was called 'Il Milione' – the man who talks in millions. He had come back from the East with fabulous, incredible tales of wealth and splendour. Even his own family turned him away from the house, until he opened his dirty, travel-stained cloak, and poured emeralds, rubies and sapphires onto the table. His name was Marco Polo, and he was the first Westerner to visit China and also to attempt to describe (in 1295) its geography, government, economic life, culture and technology, which were manifestly so much more advanced than those of early medieval Europe.

'Il Milione' became, in the Middle Ages, a byword for the incredible. Yet modern knowledge of China has vindicated the Venetian story teller. His 'black stones' mined from mountains, for example, proved to be coal. Even his detailed itineraries of Central Asia have been verified. And his perception of the strength, wealth and longevity of Chinese civilization was profound. From the thirteenth to the nineteenth century China maintained its position as the most powerful and unified world power. The thesis of this book is to examine how and why the pendulum of history which swung so visibly and decisively towards the West in the past 200 years is now beginning to return at an accelerating pace towards a twenty-first-century world dominated by the East, in wealth, population, technology and economic dynamism.

THE EAST–WEST INDEX

The East–West Index is intended to be a composite relative indicator of economic and technological progress. One of the main

Chart 1.1: The East–West Index

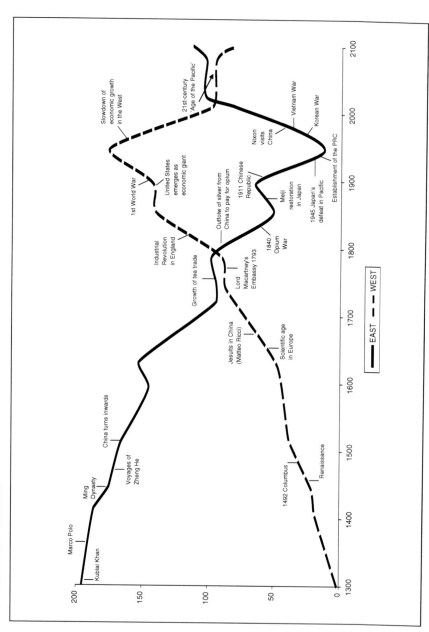

factors is the flow of capital between East and West which, before 1840, comprised a regular flow of silver from Europe to China. By contrast, in the last forty years there has been a steady annual trade deficit between the United States and Japan. For the early centuries, of course, we do not have the exact figures for levels of economic development, gross national product (GNP) or population. We can, however, make educated guesses, based on the observations made by Marco Polo and others, of the standard of living and culture in China compared with Europe. The historian Fernand Braudel, in his books *The Mediterranean (1949)* and *Civilization and Capitalism (1982)*, attempted to quantify these economic differences, notably by using price levels in different areas of the world during the Middle Ages. Thus, the author has used many different sources to reach actual historical comparisons. The overall index is bound to overweight certain factors at different times. What may be called the psychological factor in the development of certain civilizations at certain times is considered important. For example, the confidence of the early period of the Ming Dynasty, 1380 to 1450, is contrasted with the faltering leadership of the later Qing Dynasty, from 1800 onwards, which in turn may be compared with the expanding confidence of the British Empire at the same period.

Scientific discoveries and inventions and the level of national technology are an important part of the index. Before 1400 China was technologically in advance of the West and Marco Polo's astonishment at many aspects of life in China under the rule of Kublai Khan attest to this contrast. Gunpowder, paper money, printing, the quality of silk apparel, the sophistication of the culinary art, the skill in navigating and many other examples can be cited. Chart 1.1, which appears opposite, details Chinese inventions and discoveries and the time which elapsed before many of these ideas reached the West or were independently discovered in the West.

Allied to applied technology is, of course, the important factor of military power. The Chinese discovered gunpowder but did not use it for military purposes and this may be the major reason why China was consistently defeated by Western military expeditions during the nineteenth century. Skill in navigation went hand in hand with the thirst for geographical discovery and the curiosity or desire for wealth which impelled it. China's great admiral, Zheng He, sailed as far as Arabia and East Africa in the 1420s (and perhaps further), but 1433 marked the end of China's overseas expeditions. By contrast, Christopher Columbus' voyage across the Atlantic in 1492 marked the beginning of a long period of exploration and discovery by Western navigators. No greater contrast can be found between the two mentalities. Just as China closed in on itself during the later Ming period and early Manchu Dynasty, so the West's momentum was accelerating in the age of scientific discovery, the Reformation and the beginnings of capitalism in Europe.

Many scholars consider that equality between China and Europe ended in 1793 on the occasion of the British Ambassador, Lord Macartney's, visit to the Emperor Qian Long at his summer palace.

Chart 1.2: Share of China and India in global manufacturing output

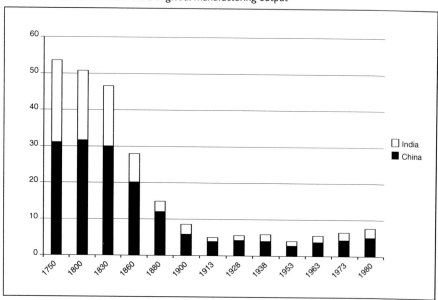

From this time on there was a steep decline in China's relative power and influence. After 1860 calculating the Asian balance becomes more complex since at that point the rapidly modernizing Japan comes into the equation. From the Meiji restoration (1868) onwards, Japan moved at extraordinary speed to strengthen its economy, its military and naval capability, and its technological potential. However, the West was also strengthened by the emergence of the United States as a great power around 1900. The turning point of Asian power and influence may be considered (again symbolically) as 1950. Firstly, because European colonial powers retreated from South-East Asia. Secondly, the end of US military occupation of Japan and the Korean War marked the beginning of the economic boom in Japan, while Mao Zedong's proclamation in Peking on 1 October 1949 that 'China has stood up' was perhaps the single most important event. China's confidence had been restored and, whether under Communism or under a freer system in the overseas Chinese communities, the Chinese would begin a generation of tremendous economic advance after 100 years of impoverishment, corrupt regimes and domination by the Western colonial powers.

The growth of Asia in the past fifty years has been astonishing and it has included both Communist nations such as China, as well as Japan and the other free Asian nations. China, under the Communists, moved rapidly to solve the age-old problem of famine. A strong, unified, central state was re-established, and this maintained a strong People's Liberation Army. In this respect, the organization of the country was akin to the early years of previous dynasties.

So, the pendulum of history has been visibly swinging back towards Asia in the past fifty years. The most obvious indicator is economic growth, which has averaged 7% per annum in Asia during the past five decades as compared to 3% in Western countries. The continuation of this trend is the basis for my forecast that Asian economies will account for more than 50% of the world's economic production within the next few years. The equation is simple. The rapid growth in population, multiplied by the growth in personal income, equals an economic boom. It also promotes political stability. Modern communications have done much to underpin this economic boom. The Boeing 747, the telephone and above all the internet have shrunk the Pacific and accelerated trade flows, between Japan and California, Hong Kong and Canada and many other countries.

Writing in 2005, the biggest change in the world has been the influence of the internet, which really only started around 1995. The investment world began to take notice and anticipate the importance of the internet in 1999–2000, with the infamous bubble in the NASDAQ, which had echoes around the world, including the Neuer Markt in Germany and some of the Japanese tech stocks. Although it was barely felt in the other Asian markets, there has been some follow-through in the number of 'dot com' companies beginning to do business in Hong Kong and other Chinese cities. The main strength of China is in its industrial manufacturing position as a low-cost competitor. The effect of the internet has been to bring this 'China price' of manufactured products directly to the consumer in

Table 1.3: The 'China price'

- Factory wages – RMB 1,000/month (US$120) rising 20% p.a.
- DVD players at US$30
- Chinese cars at US$5,000 or less
- Auto parts, foundries, violins, umbrellas and commercial airplanes
- WalMart as an agent of change
- Implications

the West. The deflationary trend in world markets in the past five years owes much to the tendency of the global market-place to come down to the lowest-price producer, which tends to be the Chinese manufacturer or Indian service provider (in the case of software). A good example was after 1 January 2005 when the last textile quotas were removed from the US import market, in which China's share jumped within a month from 16% to 60%. At the same time, the price of cotton-knit sweaters fell 45% in less than a year. Whilst this benefits global consumers, it has a rather dramatic effect of 'creative destruction' on other textile producers from North Carolina to Italy and from Mexico to Indonesia.

ASIAN RELIGIONS AND PHILOSOPHIES

The collapse of Communism in Russia and Eastern Europe in 1989–91 was not followed in Asia, where China, North Korea and Vietnam have maintained the one-party totalitarian rule of the Communist Party. However, it is difficult when visiting China today to find any sincere Marxist believers. Since Deng Xiaoping gave the signal, in Shenzhen in February 1992, that 'to get rich is glorious', the Chinese people have responded with alacrity and today the prevalent philosophy is individualistic capitalism. The social and environmental consequences of this rush to improve living standards are already visible, but the interesting question is what will fill the spiritual and moral vacuum, especially among the younger generation in China, since the collapse of Maoism as a hollow creed.

Among the most visible responses to this hunger for tradition and meaning, has been the emergence of the Falun Gong, which emerged suddenly in the late 1990s as a spiritual movement based on traditional Chinese beliefs, in opposition to the ruling Communist Party. The roots of Falun Gong are somewhat akin to the Boxer Rebellion of 1898, which was based on the cult of Chi Gong, or Chinese traditional martial arts. What was notable about Falun Gong was that it was organized over the internet and was able to stage demonstrations in various cities without warning. The authorities cracked down heavily on Falun Gong, which has gone quiet since 2002.

The economic success of Japan, Korea and to a degree Taiwan has probably owed something to the strong Confucian work ethic. The analects of Confucius advocate order, respect, hierarchy, good manners and the sacrifice of the individual for the greater good of the family or the community. The most important values in Confucian philosophy are respect for age and seniority, and filial duty.

Both Buddhism and Christianity are flourishing underground in China without posing a significant threat to the rule of the Communist Party. However, Christianity has never succeeded in converting more than about 1% of the population in China or Japan. There is a striking contrast in South Korea, where over 25% of the population are practising Christians, which has had an important influence on the political and social life of that country. Apart from Korea, only the Philippines has a dominant Catholic majority. There are however important and well financed missionary efforts coming from Hong Kong to foster the growth of the underground churches in China and this may in the future have an effect on the mainland (the Taiping rebellion of 1851–64 originated in the belief of the leader of the rebellion that he was the younger brother of Jesus Christ).

In 1991 we estimated that there were 50 million Muslims in China, and there are about 70 million now. Whilst it is very hard to be sure of any number, the minority populations in central Asia, especially Xinjiang, such as the Uighurs, are still practising Muslims, and on China's western borders Kazakhstan, Usbekistan, Kyrgyzstan and Tajikistan are all essentially Muslim nations. Following the 9/11 attacks, China took advantage of the strong anti-terrorist mood to crack down on the Uighurs and the western separatists. But its need for good relations with the oil-producing countries of the Middle East may moderate this domestic policy in the future.

There are also of course major Muslim populations in Malaysia and in Indonesia, where the Chinese minorities are vulnerable to any fundamentalist movement.

ASIAN TECHNOLOGY

The important part of the East–West Index as a composite indicator is how technology and the impact of scientific inventions have affected people's everyday lives, in China compared with the West. Marco Polo was impressed by the smooth organization of life under Kublai Khan and the arrangements for transport, money, food and clothing, agriculture and engineering. I have again included an abbreviated table to show the Chinese inventions and discoveries and the long time lag before similar discoveries were made in the West.

One example of this Chinese lead in technology up to the early 1400s was the theory espoused in *1421: The Year China Discovered The World* (Menzies, 2002) that Chinese fleets had explored not only the Indian Ocean but had gone as far afield as the Atlantic and the New World nearly a century before Columbus. This was owing to their superior technology in navigation and ship-building.

In the past fifty years the world has become a much more level playing field owing to the speed with which new patents and technologies are adopted and manufactured globally, especially in the last ten years since the arrival of the internet. Japan and Korea very rapidly overtook the United States in semi-conductor technology and production. Now China too has become a large producer of integrated circuits, initially for its own industrial needs and for consumer electrical products, but eventually also for export.

The essential point to emphasize is that China is no longer just copying and imitating Western or Japanese know-how. China will (on the evidence of its past history) innovate and invent many new products, not only in the fields of electronics and computers, but also in the fields of medicine and bio-technology. There has already been a widespread fashion for adopting Chinese herbal medicines in the West as part of the general trend towards homoeopathic remedies.

What we may expect to see in the next twenty years is a surge in Chinese medical research, which has few of the ethical constraints

Table 1.4 – Chinese inventions and discoveries and time lags before recognition or adoption in the West

Discovery/Invention	Year Discovered	Years before Adoption in the West
The iron plough	600 BC	2,200
Efficient horse harness – trace	400 BC	500
Recognition of sunspots as solar phenomena	400 BC	2,000
Quantitative cartography	200 AD	1,300
The Mercator map-projection	1000 AD	600
Cast iron	400 BC	1,700
Manufacture of steel from cast iron	200 BC	2,000
Deep drilling for natural gas	100 BC	1,900
The suspension bridge	100 AD	1,800
Lacquer, the first plastic	1300 BC	3,200
Petroleum and natural gas as fuel	400 BC	2,300
Paper	200 BC	1,400
Porcelain	300 AD	1,500
Matches	577 AD	1,000
Chess	600 AD	500
Printing – movable type	1045 AD	400
Paper money	900 AD	850
Circulation of blood	600 BC	1,800
Circadian rhythms in the human body	200 BC	2,150
Diabetes discovered by urine analysis	700 AD	1,000

that have sometimes held back US medical research. A recent UK science mission to Asia concluded that:

> Researchers in China, South Korea and Singapore are as talented as their Western counterparts, they are probably better funded and equipped. The perspective is more long term in all three countries. The challenge to Western pre-eminence in stem cell science from China, Singapore and South Korea is real. Where stem cell research in China is unique is in the drive to the clinic. There is much less resistance than would be met in the West, pursuing experimental therapies with clinical practice.

A recent example reported in the press in January 2005 was of a fight in a Chinese restaurant where a chopstick was pushed deep into the patient's skull. The neurosurgeon in Shanghai was able to remove fresh brain tissue and culture neural stem cells to transplant back into the brain with the patient making a remarkable recovery. Many of the cures in the next fifty years for cancer, heart disease, Parkinson's and diabetes may come from this 'no holds barred' pioneering medical effort in China.

When the Chinese Prime Minister Wen Jiabao visited London in May 2004 he gave a speech to a group of British businessmen, saying that one of the key trends would be patents and inventions discovered at British universities, but manufactured at Chinese factories. One of the keys therefore to the Eastern dominance of the pendulum will be a scientific and technological lead, although, once again, we in the West may expect to benefit as much from scientific innovation in the Chinese world as from its economic success.

2

The Roots of Chinese Culture

In this section I will attempt to summarize some key points about China and the Chinese to provide some background for my analysis of Chinese economic history, the success of today's overseas Chinese and their underlying business culture.

Traditionally, the family rather than the individual, or the state, has formed the basic unit in Chinese society. In China the rule of law is of less importance than in the United States and Europe, where conflicting elements in a society such as church and state, capital and labour, government and business, are balanced by the law. By contrast, in traditional China personal virtues of loyalty and honesty, sincerity and benevolence, backed up by the family system provided the basis for commercial contact. Law was a necessary tool of administration but personal family relationships were the foundation of society. Many of the problems of modernization in Chinese society today result from this aspect of Chinese culture.

From early times the Chinese have considered the unity of the state of prime importance. Unaware of the great cultures of the West they considered China the centre of civilization surrounded on all sides by barbarians. They called their country *Zhongguo*, literally the 'central country', commonly translated as the 'Middle Kingdom'. Zhongguo is still the Chinese name for their land. They looked down on all foreigners as being inferior and uncivilized and many of the problems of early diplomatic contacts with the West stemmed from this notion of the Middle Kingdom.

The Chinese writing system has linked many of the peoples of the Asian continent. All literate Chinese, even if they speak mutually unintelligible dialects, can read the same books and feel that written Chinese is their own language. The linguistic map of East Asia shows the full extent of the influence of China or rather the Sinitic languages. It does not clearly indicate, however, that both the Korean and Japanese languages, though very different in origin, borrowed their systems of writing from China and are thus culturally tied to China.

The teachings of Confucius (551–479 BC) still have a major influence on society in East Asia today. Confucius, like his Greek contemporaries, Plato and Socrates, was essentially a teacher of ethics. His main thesis was that good government was a matter of personal morality. He insisted that the first duty of a statesman was to set a proper example of sound ethical conduct. He argued that the rule of virtue and the contentment of the people, rather than power, should be the true measure of political success. His ideal ruler was a *Junzi*, which is usually translated as 'the superior man' or 'gentleman'. He placed a great emphasis on ritual and etiquette and believed people should foster inner attitudes through the practice of external forms. He set the East Asian pattern of compromise, of seeking the middle path. His emphasis on moderation, balance and harmony has moulded the Asian psyche. Confucianism eventually became the accepted wisdom of successive generations of scholars and officials while the emphasis on learning and the establishment of the examination system opened the political arena to all people of talent from whatever social background.

During the past 2,000 years of Chinese history a pattern is discernible of a new dynasty starting with a dynamic emperor asserting a vigorous rule over the empire and maintaining the unity of China, establishing a strong army, collecting the taxes and settling frontier disputes. Usually within 100 years, according to the pattern, government begins to show a gradual deterioration. The decline starts with a failure to collect taxes and results in financial problems in the civil service and the army, with increasingly hostile tribes on the northern frontier of China. This was true of the Ming Dynasty. It was also true of the Qing Dynasty. The question is, how will the Communist Dynasty, which began in 1949 with Mao Zedong, reflect the pattern of China's dynastic history?

A historian will always hesitate before saying this is a new era, with a new set of factors. My contention is that China remains the same. The Cultural Revolution of 1966–76 was compared by the historian Trevor-Roper to the Boxer Rebellion of 1898–1900. In both cases the Western legations in Peking were besieged by huge crowds of students and soldiers waving anti-Western placards. The opening-up of China during the 1980s may also be compared to the situation in the late-nineteenth century when China opened up to Western trade and missionaries for the last time, though only under the compulsion of superior Western military power. The pendulum swings back and forth between allowing Westerners in and expelling them – the yin and yang of the Middle Kingdom mentality and international awareness and openness. It may be argued that Deng Xiaoping's most decisive contribution to the future of China was his decision in 1979, following his visit to the United States, to send 50,000 of China's brightest and best young people to study in the West, mainly in America. One of the consequences of this decision was the upsurge of students peacefully demonstrating for democracy in Tiananmen Square in May 1989. My own belief is that in the longer term China will not again, in the next fifty years, turn in on itself, since it now has a Western-educated, internationally minded, young elite who are becoming the rulers of China.

But the dynastic pattern may well survive. Corruption, which has grown so rapidly in China during the economic boom of the past twenty years, was also the result of the old Chinese tradition of ensuring favours for members of one's family. It will undoubtedly continue to be a characteristic of the way China does business with the outside world and it may well become, in the twenty-first century, one of the leading causes of the downfall of this Communist Dynasty, as it has been of previous dynasties. Finally, corruption and lack of moral integrity will leave a vacuum of power at the heart of the empire.

CHINESE EMIGRATION

The first Chinese emigrants started to leave China before 1400 AD (although there is evidence of Chinese merchant shipping in the Indian Ocean as early as 900 AD) and it is around this time that the first historical voyages of Chinese trading fleets are recorded. The longest and most famous series of seven expeditions headed by the great eunuch, Admiral Zheng He, between 1405 and 1433, reached as far as Zanzibar and the East African and Arabian coasts. Already at that date there was a well established Chinese community on the west coast of Malaysia at Malacca. Malacca is of great symbolic historical importance as the meeting place of East and West for medieval trade and the exchange of ideas, including the spread of Islam into the East Indies. It served as the base for St. Francis Xavier's missionary voyages to the Philippines, Macao and Japan. It seems likely, therefore, that the majority of Chinese emigrants going to the *Nanyang* or South Seas would have passed this way, through Malacca, and into both Malaysia and Indonesia. Some of the contemporary population of Singapore are descendants of the so-called Baba Chinese of Malacca. Some of the largest communities of overseas Chinese populations are those in Malaysia, Singapore and Indonesia. Burma (Myanmar) and Thailand, sharing a border with China, would also have received direct migration overland.

The provinces of China from which most overseas Chinese today originate are Guangdong, centred on the city of Canton and the Pearl River estuary, and Fujian, from which came the settlers of Taiwan, the Fujianese or Hokkien people. From Canton, apart from the Cantonese, there were minorities such as the Hakka; and Chiu Chow, who in the nineteenth century were mainly 'coolies' from the area around the port of Swatow (Shantou). Among today's Chinese population in Bangkok the majority are Chiu Chow. They are renowned for their skill in rice-trading and banking and famous among the Chiu Chow community are the Soponpanich family of Bangkok Bank (originally surnamed Chin). Another celebrated Chiu Chow is Li Ka Shing, Hong Kong's leading real-estate entrepreneur and one of the world's richest men. The Hakka were a thrifty, hard-working, mountain people from the north-eastern part of Guangdong Province (originally from northern China) who moved not only to Hong Kong but also to Malaysia and Indonesia. The Fujianese or those who speak the Hokkien dialect predominate in the population of Singapore.

Mention should also be made of the smaller but highly influential community of Shanghainese people who emigrated in the 1940s, some to Hong Kong but others to Taiwan and the United States. They have been especially successful in the textile, shipping and banking fields and included in their number were leading businessmen such as Sir Y. K. Pao. Many United States Chinese businessmen, scholars and scientists are also Shanghainese in origin, such as An Wang, the architect I. M. Pei and a number of Nobel prize-winning physicists.

It may seem surprising that none of the interior provinces of China and very few of the northern provinces around Peking and in Manchuria provided any (or at least very few) of the Chinese emigrant population. Part of the answer seems to be that population pressure in the south was greater and so encouraged emigration. But it is also true to say that the grip of Mandarin culture and bureaucracy was less strong among the southern Chinese, who were and are more motivated towards trade and the ideas of the Western world, than towards scholarship and Chinese tradition.

It is important to appreciate the subtle differences between these different overseas Chinese communities since these differences persist so strongly in present-day business relationships and practices. In describing the dialects Cantonese, Hakka, Chiu Chow, Fukianese, Shanghainese – for example – it should not be forgotten that most educated Chinese also speak Mandarin. In Taiwan, particularly, Mandarin is widely spoken although the local dialect is closer to that of Fujian province. In Singapore, also, the government has made strenuous efforts to promote the use of Mandarin as well as English as a national language. However, in the many Chinese restaurants in North America and Europe the language mainly spoken is Cantonese. The Cantonese are some of the most dynamic emigrants, the entrepreneurs and traders of the Chinese world. Nowhere can this be seen more clearly than in Hong Kong, where the population is 98% Cantonese, but this is equally true of Canton, and the other towns on the Pearl River estuary, which are much closer in spirit to Hong Kong than to other provinces in China. The common bond is the Cantonese language and the Cantonese people, who are famous not only for their cuisine, but also for their energy and skill in commerce.

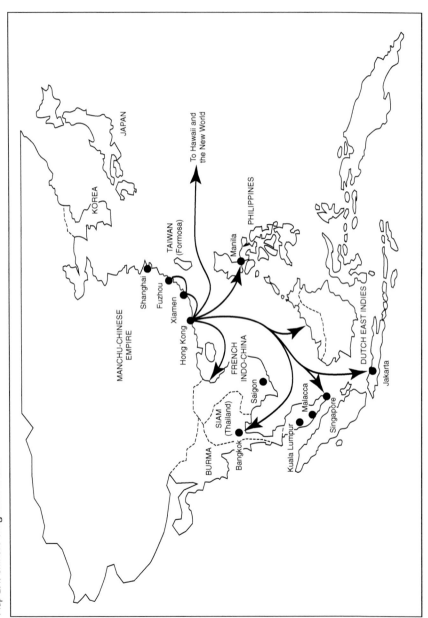

Map 2.1: Chinese emigration in 1900

The main destinations of the Chinese emigrants in the period 1860–1930 were Singapore and Malaysia, Thailand and Burma (mainly arriving overland), Indonesia and the Philippines. The settlement of Chinese traders in South-East Asia alone pre-dates Western colonialism. The main influx started in the nineteenth century, stemming from the local demand for coolie labour and the breakdown of order in China following the Taiping rebellion in the 1850s. Today, the overseas Chinese in these countries mostly stand on the periphery of politics but at the core of business life. There are exceptions to this rule, however, particularly in the Philippines and Thailand, where assimilation has been greatest.

If we look at the size of the Chinese population in each country it is, of course, largest in Singapore (about 75%), the only country where the government is dominated by the Chinese. In Malaysia, the Chinese are in a minority, accounting for 35% of the population, compared with about 55% of Malays. The Malays dominate the political scene and the Chinese dominate the business world. The minority is even smaller in the highly populated Indonesian archipelago. None the less, it is estimated that 80% of the country's commerce is in the hands of the Chinese. In both Jakarta in 1998 and Kuala Lumpur in 1969, there were fierce anti-Chinese riots and pogroms, so that the insecurity of the Chinese minority populations is founded on events well within living memory.

The story is very different in Thailand, which, being predominantly Buddhist, is a tolerant and easy-going country which has assimilated its Chinese population as it has other foreigners. In fact, because of this long-established policy of assimilation, it is almost impossible to ascertain who is Chinese. A rough estimate would be that the Chinese community accounts for between 5% and 10% of the total Thai population. Within Bangkok itself almost every major company, with notable exceptions such as Siam Cement, is dominated by Chinese management. Even more apparent are the strong interconnections of Chinese family businesses in these different countries, i.e. between branches of families in Bangkok and Hong Kong, between Taipei and Singapore, and between Jakarta and Kuala Lumpur. Most of the international trade in South-East Asia, therefore, goes through Chinese trading companies and Chinese banks.

Another interesting case is that of the Philippines, to which there was also a considerable amount of Chinese emigration in the late nineteenth century. There, too, the centre of economic power has shifted inexorably from the Spanish Mestizo (Spanish-Malay elite) to the Filipino Chinese who, although accounting for only 3% of the population, control as much as 60% of the country's banking and commerce. The local Chinese are more racially exclusive than the native Filipinos. Their names are often unknown to other Filipino business people and most of their foreign trade is conducted with relatives and clansmen in other countries.

In general, however, the tendency of the Chinese in the past has been to concentrate on business. Each family's experience of deprivation, starvation and refugee status from a Communist regime is too recent to allow anything else. The tendency has been to do well for your family first and let others worry about political problems.

However, all this has begun to change rapidly. The ending of martial law in Taiwan in mid-1987 was symbolic not only of the eclipse of the Chiang family's power but of the emergence of a new democratic opposition. In Manila and Seoul the old authoritarian ideas have become rapidly outdated. The younger Chinese population is both more educated and more politically aware than their parents. Much of this might, perhaps, be traced to the influence of US university education on the younger generation in the past twenty years. It has, of course, had a profound effect on China itself where the decision of Deng Xiaoping, after 1979, not only to open China's doors to the world but, more importantly, to send China's best young people to study in Western universities, has proved to have had a more revolutionary effect than its architect had expected. There is no doubt that in the coming decade this political awareness and this new-found idealism in the Chinese younger generation will grow and become a more powerful factor throughout the Chinese world.

In 1965 the United States took what proved to be a historic decision under President Lyndon Johnson. The Oriental Exclusion Act of 1884 which, for more than eighty years, had banned Chinese

Table 2.2: The Chinese diaspora

	Population (million)
Taiwan	22
Hong Kong	7
Malaysia	6
Singapore	3
Indonesia	7
Thailand	6
Philippines	4
Other Asia	5
United States	2.5
Canada	1
Australia	0.25
United Kingdom	0.75
Others	1
Total (approx)	**65**

immigration into the United States was finally repealed and in its place the present quota system was set up. What this meant in practice was that for all Asian countries there would be a certain number of entrants allowed in automatically each year, excluding, of course, those with family ties and business immigrants.

Compared with 1901–20 when 75% of immigrants into the United States came from Europe and only 10% from Asia, the early 1980s witnessed a shift to about 50% from Asia and 20% from Europe. The balance of 30% came mainly from Mexico and Latin America. The number of Asian Americans has climbed rapidly to exceed 6 million today. Of these, the largest ethnic groups, according to the United States census, are the Filipinos, the Chinese and the Vietnamese. A large number of refugees have also been taken in from Indo-China since the ending of the Vietnam War in 1975. Of the immigrants from the Philippines, Thailand, Malaysia and Indonesia, a large percentage are of Chinese origin. They also tend to be the people with the most education, skills and financial backing.

The numbers in themselves are, therefore, less important than the results of a highly motivated and educated group whose success, especially in business and in the academic world, has been out of all proportion to their size. It should be very clear, however, that the effect of this American policy change forty years ago has been nothing but positive for the United States. What is very hard to measure is the total economic or cultural gain. Nobody knows how many dollars are invested in the United States each year from Taiwan, for example. Yet it is these invisible factors which have the greatest long-term impact.

Table 2.2 gives details of the 'Chinese diaspora', showing an approximate estimate of the size of the overseas Chinese populations around the world. A conservative figure of 65 million has been reached which would represent about 5% of the population of mainland China today, at 1.3 billion. This compares, for example, with an estimate of 15 to 20 million overseas Indians compared to 1 billion in India itself. The Chinese, proportionately, have a far greater and more widespread influence, especially in South-East Asia and increasingly on the western coast of Canada and the United States.

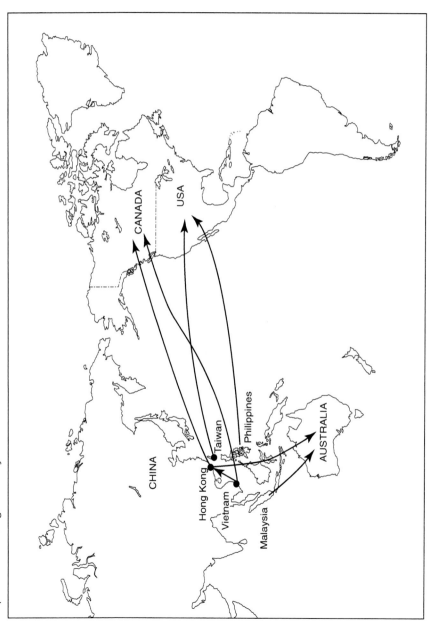

Map 2.3 – Chinese emigration today

THE CHINESE FAMILY

Neither the nation nor the company but the family is the basic unit of Chinese society. Just as if we want to understand the success of Japan we must study the Japanese corporation, so, too, to understand overseas Chinese business corporations, we must study the Chinese family. Apart from its economic importance there is also much that the West, with its high divorce rate, single-parent families and neglected senior citizens, can learn from the cultural and ethical traditions of the family in Chinese tradition.

The main ideas preached by Confucius were the principles of hierarchy, order and harmony within the society. The loyalty owed by a subject to the emperor parallels that owed by a son to his father. Chinese stories are full of examples of filial piety. A modern example of this is Frank Ching's excellent book *Ancestors (1988)*, in which he traces the genealogy of the Ching family for 1,000 years, back to a poet of the tenth century. He also recounts a number of moving stories of self-sacrifice illustrating this virtue of filial piety. To quote the philosopher Mencius, 'There are three ways of being an unfilial son. The worst is to have no heir.' In fact, so precisely did Confucius lay down the rules of social behaviour that each individual knew exactly his or her position within the family and, therefore, within society and his or her duty to each member of it. The hierarchy is based on generation, age and sex.

Thus there are five human relationships in which human beings are involved, as follows:

1. Emperor/subject;
2. Father/son;
3. Older brother/younger brother;
4. Husband/wife;
5. Friend/friend.

Father/son relationships are central to the success of a continuing family business and this is still valid in overseas Chinese businesses today, where it is rare for a son to take any important decisions while his father is alive. Nothing is more misleading than to be told that the family patriarch has 'retired'. Singapore's Mr. Lee has now become the 'Minister Mentor' having been the 'Senior Minister'.

The individual within the Chinese family is of far less importance than in the West. It is not the family which exists in order to support the individual but rather the individual that exists in order to continue the family: the reverse of Western thinking. For example, it is common that the brightest boy in the family, even if he is not the oldest, will be financed through college by the family on the clear, but unspoken, understanding that his subsequent lifetime earnings as a lawyer or a doctor, for instance, will be channelled back into the family's joint savings. A decision by the family to go into a certain kind of business, to buy a property or even to make an arranged marriage are all communal family decisions, taken together but ultimately obeying the wishes of the paterfamilias.

Family and kinship relationships are very closely tied into overseas Chinese business activities. The family will not do business with people they do not know – no one deals with strangers. Business relationships are always, to some degree, personal relationships. Thus, business organization is built on the basis of kinship. A Hong Kong merchant would feel more comfortable in dealing with a second cousin living in Bangkok, for example, than in dealing with someone from a different area who lives next door to him. James Michener's story of the Yee family in his novel *Hawaii*, provides a good description of the Chinese family business.

The most essential asset in the Chinese business world is a good reputation. This may take years to acquire and can be lost very rapidly. In order to start a business one needs capital, of course, but that in itself is not enough. One must have *Xinyong*, which means having a good reputation (and credit rating) with other members of the same profession. This is another reason why, in traditional China and in overseas Chinese communities today, legal contracts have been considered to be of little importance. In traditional China, the family have always come before the law. There is an almost universal Chinese aversion to lawsuits and arbitration. Personal relationships account for much more than contractual relationships. Threats to one's reputation, along with community sanctions, appear to have been sufficient incentives to act honourably and to maintain good faith.

If we try to sum up the style and essence of overseas Chinese business we can identify the following four characteristics:

1. Flexible decision-making by one strong individual.
2. Strong family control and connections to overseas cousins.
3. Highly informed financial planning (though unstructured in the Western sense).
4. Reliance on personal trust rather than legal contracts.

The importance of understanding Chinese business culture is underlined by the fact that much of the business of the Pacific Rim today is in the hands of overseas Chinese companies. Long before the large Japanese trading companies became so powerful, Chinese merchants and their family networks had already established an economic system throughout South-East Asia. It would be impossible to prove statistically but it is estimated that 75% of all trade in Indonesia, Malaysia, Singapore and the Philippines today goes through firms controlled by overseas Chinese.

Parallel to the view that the family is more important than the individual is the very different Chinese idea of time. Because the individual's life is of less importance, so a longer-term view can be taken of investment decisions, which may be meditated for many years. The most eloquent description of the individual's place in time is as follows:

Descent is a unity, a rope which began somewhere back in the remote past, and which stretches on to the infinite future. The rope at any one time may be thicker or thinner according to the number of strands (families) or fibres (male individuals) which exist, but so long as one fibre remains the rope is there. The fibres at any one point are not just fibres, they are the representatives of the rope as a whole. The living individual is the personification of all his forebears and of his descendants yet unborn. He exists by virtue of his ancestors, and his descendants exist only through him, the rope stretches from Infinity to Infinity passing over a razor which is the Present. If the rope is cut, both ends fall away from the middle and the rope is no more. If the man alive now dies without heir, the whole continuum of ancestors and unborn descendants dies with him.

There is a close link between this sense of family continuity and the importance of land in Chinese thinking. There is a continuous effort to secure wealth in the form of land. Land is very rarely sold. Most overseas Chinese people still have today a clear idea of the village from which their families originated. There is a strong pull back towards this motherland. The greatest virtue of land is its inherent illiquidity. It is difficult to sell in a hurry. Again, the emphasis is on the family's interest, not the individual's over a longer period of time.

Education is another basic element in Chinese family thinking. In traditional China, learning was the road to power and prestige which could be attained through competition in the civil-service examinations. To be a scholar was to have an entry to the civil service and the power and security that went with official posts in imperial China. In a sense, both land and education are linked to the Chinese search for security. Until very recently in many countries of South-East Asia overseas Chinese were prohibited from owning land, therefore business skills and education replaced property ownership as the main route to wealth. The thirst for land and the thirst for education can both be traced to the insecurity which characterizes many overseas Chinese communities. Hong Kong is only one example and in Indonesia and Malaysia fear and discrimination motivate overseas Chinese to look around the Pacific Rim for suitable investment opportunities, especially for real estate in North America.

3

Differing Responses to the West

In assessing the potential risk and reward for investors in each Asian country I believe there is probably no single, more reliable indicator to the attitude of these countries to foreign investors than the history of their response to foreigners and to Western influences during the era of the opening-up of Asia between 1850 and 1900. The sections which follow give a country-by-country description of these Asian responses to foreigners.

CHINA

Our study must begin with China. Although the first European contacts with China had begun with the Portuguese as early as 1517 and trade had continued through Macau during the eighteenth century – although, too, the Russian penetration of Siberia had led to a succession of embassies in the late seventeenth and eighteenth centuries – it was finally the British East India Company, with its trading post at Canton, which provoked the opening-up of China to global commerce. The first Anglo-Chinese War, 1839–42, known as the Opium War, was the catalyst for this momentous change. A war that was precipitated by the Qing government's justifiable efforts to suppress the pernicious, contraband trade in opium, was won by the superior fire power of British warships and followed by the 'unequal treaties' that gave Westerners special privileges in China, including the granting in perpetuity of Hong Kong island to the British.

With the benefit of hindsight, conflict was probably inevitable, given on the one hand the outdated Chinese view of the outside world as a series of small nations bearing tribute to the Middle Kingdom and, on the other hand, Europe, led by England in the midst of its industrial revolution, with a strong military and naval power pushing aggressively to pursue business opportunities in the East. The large discrepancy in power relations led to a great change in China's relations with the outside world. Not only China's relative military weakness but also the West's ideas of scientific learning, individual freedom and economic growth all helped to make such a change inevitable.

In demanding diplomatic equality and commercial opportunity, Britain represented all the other Western powers. The Treaty of Nanking of 1842 abolished the Chinese monopoly of foreign trade at Canton, ceded Hong Kong to Britain and opened five ports to British residents and trade – Canton, Amoy, Foochow, Ningpo and Shanghai. It was the first of a number of further 'treaties' signed in the following decade with the French, the Americans and other Western powers. Under the terms of the treaty the British were granted rights of residence in the treaty ports and extraterritoriality (protection from Chinese laws). China ceded these privileges to Westerners under duress. A similar experience occurred when Commodore Perry arrived in Japan in 1853–4 but with very different results (see following section).

The attitude of the Chinese authorities to foreign merchants and missionaries did not really undergo any change in the next fifty years, as the Anglo-French war with China in 1858–60 (the Second Opium War) and the Boxer Rebellion of 1898–1900 were to prove. It was only after the Anglo-French capture of Tientsin and Peking in 1860 that the Chinese government finally accepted the posting of Western ambassadors to the imperial city, again under threat of force. The suppression of the Taiping rebellion in 1864 was achieved with Western help, led by General Gordon. The Manchu Dynasty was thus given a new lease of life as China opened up for international trade and international diplomatic relations. The creation of the Chinese Imperial Maritime Customs Service under the leadership of Sir Robert Hart was the prime example of the acceptance by the Chinese authorities of the need for Western experts. The modernization drive of the late nineteenth century continued under the slogan: 'Chinese learning for fundamentals, Western learning for practical needs'.

Only after the founding of the Chinese Republic in 1911 (and then only in the late 1920s and early 1930s) for a brief period could China's potential for building a modern financial economy be observed. In the late 1980s and early 1990s this potential may have begun to be finally realized as bond markets and stockmarkets were established in the PRC, and China's vast pool of domestic savings began to be channelled towards the country's industrialization needs.

JAPAN

Japan's response to the West was very different from that of China. No wars were fought, no smuggling trade developed and no territory was lost. There was certainly a decade of domestic power struggle but out of it soon emerged a radical, new political system under which Japan moved rapidly to become a modern power by 1900.

Why did Japan react so differently from China? The Japanese had very different attitudes towards the outside world. The Chinese, long accustomed to the idea that the Middle Kingdom was the unique land of civilization, did not believe that there was much of value to be learnt from 'barbarians' and could not understand that this was a serious challenge to their national security. The Japanese, on the other hand, with their own sense of separate identity and their acute awareness of China, could understand the European system of equal and independent states. Well aware of all they had learnt over the ages from China, and even from Korea and India, they could readily see that there was much of great importance to be learnt from the West. Too accustomed to thinking of China as far larger, much older and more advanced than Japan, they had no supreme sense of cultural superiority, but rather a fear of inferiority. Thus, when menaced by the West, they did not look with disdain but rather with that combination of fear, resentment and narrow pride that one associates with nationalism.

Japan, too, was a much smaller country, in which a new Western idea could spread and develop very quickly. As one Chinese scholar (Prof. Hwang Yueh Chin) has expressed it, 'Japan was like a glass of water in which a drop of ink would immediately discolour the whole. China was a vast pool ...' in which ideas would spread very slowly, if at all.

Commodore Perry's arrival in July 1853 was at first strongly resisted. Even after the demonstration of US naval power had forced the signing of the Treaty of Kanagawa in 1854 and led to the opening of two small ports to American ships, the *samurai* lords or *daimyo*, especially in the south of Japan (Satsuma in southern Kuyshu and Choshu at the western tip of Honshu, in particular), continued to resist Western influence strongly for the next twenty years. The government slogans of 'honour the Emperor' and 'expel the barbarian' were the rallying cries. A civil war between the old *shogunate* in Kyoto and the provincial *daimyo*, mainly in Choshu and Satsuma, resulted in the 1860s in the final collapse of the Tokugowa *shogunate* in 1868. In the mean time, the Satsuma *samurai* in Kagoshima had learnt the lesson about the inadequacy of traditional Japanese military power when the English navy bombarded the city in August 1863 in retaliation for the assassination of an English trader in the province. Satsuma made an indemnity payment of £25,000 but also developed a respect for and interest in the British navy. It immediately set about procuring Western ships with British aid, thus laying the foundation for what was to grow into the Imperial Japanese Navy.

Such flexibility and willingness to learn new ideas was also at the root of the amazing saga of the Meiji Restoration. No non-Western country has ever effected such a complete and mainly peaceful political revolution in such a short time so successfully as Japan between 1868 and 1900. It was effected by a small group of young men of *samurai* origin, who, having removed the *shogun*, restored the Meiji emperor to power. Appearance and reality, however, were quite different. The Meiji emperor was a mere figurehead.

The power rested with the oligarchs such as Kido, Okubo, Saigo and Ito Hirobumi (1841–1909) who effectively ruled Japan for the first forty years of the modern era. They were determined to modernize Japan and to make it a power equal to the West. Knowledge was to be sought throughout the world so as to strengthen the foundations of imperial rule. Japan was to be modernized and strengthened through the use of Western knowledge because the only defence against the West lay in the creation of a rich country and a strong military adapting Western technology.

In this spirit, the reforming group of Meiji oligarchs proceeded to borrow the best from other Western countries – from Britain the navy and the railway system, from France the military, from Prussia the educational system, from the United States a system of national banking, and so on. Probably the most revolutionary step was the conscription law of 1873, making all men, regardless of social background, liable for three years of active military service. In addition, universal education and literacy were steadily established. The finances of the new regime were put in order within fifteen years with very little dependence on foreign borrowing. Land reform was carried out and the old feudal system effectively abolished. A new political constitution was put in place by 1880, based on the most up-to-date European models, with an upper house of peers, a national assembly, or diet, with 300 elected representatives and a ministerial system of government, under a prime minister and cabinet all answerable in theory to the supreme authority of the emperor. Despite the initial teething problems with this radical democratic reform, Japan had succeeded by the early twentieth century in its aim of creating a modern state and a military power which demonstrated its effectiveness in both the Sino-Japanese War of 1894–5 and, even more strikingly, in its defeat of imperial Russia in the war of 1904–5. Meanwhile, the economic modernization of Japan had proceeded rapidly. Many Western analysts today seeking to understand the secrets of the Japanese economic miracle since 1945 may well find the foundations of this success in the Meiji period.

The whole foundation for Japan's modern industrial development was formed during the last thirty years of the nineteenth century. In fact, the financial problems of the new Meiji government resulted in a policy of economic retrenchment by which, in November 1880, the government sold all non-strategic government industries, such as shipbuilding, armaments, textiles, steel and transport. Most were sold at very low prices to leading businesspeople or even government officials and for ten years did not show any great profitability (like the privatizations in Europe of the 1980s and 1990s). Nevertheless, this initial step contributed to the eventual concentration of much of Japanese industry in the hands of a few giant companies, the *zaibatsu*. With exceptions such as Mitsui and Sumitomo, they were rarely the old trading houses. More often they were successful *samurai* entrepreneurs such as Iwasaki Yataro, who founded Mitsubishi and developed the first major shipping line. Another example was Shibusawa Etichi, who founded the Osaka spinning mill and was the father of Japan's modern textile industry.

By the 1890s Japanese exports had commenced, led by the cotton-spinning industry, which employed about 63% of all factory workers at that time. Simultaneously, the Nippon Yusen Kaisha (NYK) Shipping Line was founded under Mitsubishi leadership in 1885. An early pattern was established of government and industry co-operating in leading strategic industries and also of vertical integration – for example, from the cotton-spinning factory to the international shipping line – which was in time to make Japan's export machine – known as 'Japan Inc.' – a fearsomely efficient competitor in the twentieth-century world.

From the beginning however, Japan's economic growth depended on exports. Foreign trade was necessary as a source of raw materials, especially minerals and fuels, and also of machinery imports. However, the percentage of foreign trade accounted for in Japan's economy as a whole remained low and, relative to European countries, remains low to this day. Japan's large population of 120 million and its enormous domestic consumption is still a key to the growth of its economy. It should never be forgotten that Japan was isolated from the entire world for over 200 years from 1640 to 1853. During that period its economy, its culture and its internal transport system all developed rapidly without any foreign help. Many of the characteristics of modern Japan were set during the Tokugowa period. However, it is the remarkable story of the forty years from 1870 to 1910 during which the Meiji oligarchs led Japan into the modern world, politically and economically, which really gives the best understanding of how Japan is ruled politically and how Japan handles the Western challenge today as it did a century ago.

There is still today, as in the 1880s, a tremendous appetite for Western novelties, fashions and new products. But it is also true to say that in most leading product markets, the market share (including Western banks'), rarely exceeds 2% or 3%. Such is the stranglehold of the large domestic corporations, the *zaibatsu* or, as they have been known since 1945, the *keiretsu*, that it is rare for a Western company, even IBM, to gain a leading market share.

JAPANESE ECONOMY 1900–40

There was a boom in the Japanese economy in the early part of the century which depended very little on foreign investment. The population grew from 43 million in 1900 to 73 million in 1940. Domestic consumption was important but there was also export demand for cottons and bicycles and other light-industrial products. Government expenditure increased rapidly in the military sphere, creating a domestic market for Japan's heavy industries before their products could be sold in the West. The First World War in Europe also increased demand for Japanese manufactured goods which, for the first time, expanded into other Asian countries. By 1920 Japan had become a creditor nation with gold resources of more than ¥2 billion – a six-fold increase in six years. This was followed by high inflation and a credit collapse during the 1920s. It is very interesting to note that the great Kanto earthquake of 1923 did not adversely affect Japan's economy. In fact it set off a construction boom and this might be the pattern of any future such event in Japan, despite the large property losses which could result.

During the 1920s and 1930s a key indicator in tracking the health of Japan's economy is to look at the prices of rice and silk, which were the major basic products of Japanese agriculture and also major exports. Even today rice is not merely symbolic, but essential to land values and to political life in Japan. It was the perceived vulnerability of

Japan's economy to this basic shortage of raw materials, oil, food and other commodities, which led directly to the decision to expand into China and after 1941 to the Pacific War. Major targets of Japan's thrust south were the oilfields of Indonesia. Today there is close economic co-operation between Japan and Indonesia, effectively guaranteeing Japanese industry a steady, cheap supply of liquid natural gas (LNG).

The *zaibatsu* system was the key to Japan's economic development both before and (in a less visible form) after the war. During the 1920s and 1930s Mitsui and Mitsubishi were probably the two largest private economic empires in the world, each having more than 100 companies within their conglomerates and employing about one million people in Japan and outside. They were involved in mining, manufacturing, trading, shipping and banking. At the centre each was tightly controlled by a single family. But the policy of these giant combines was also closely intertwined with Japan's national policy and strategic interests. The capital investment which they were able to make in new technologies derived from their enormous size and financial strength. In 1945 the Americans saw the destruction of these military-industrial complexes as one of their main aims. However, these giant combines had positive effects too and the strength of the Japanese economy today still owes a great deal to the core strength of these *keiretsu* groups. However, in Japan today, as in 1930, more than half of the manufacturing labour force is employed in small businesses. Unlike the Chinese, the core unit of Japanese society tends to be not the family but the company, whether large or small, encompassing all aspects of life, somewhat like the old *samurai* military units.

Japan, like Siam, was able to absorb Western ideas without losing its own unique culture. The achievement was the more remarkable when it is seen how rapidly it was effected on other levels during the Meiji period. In particular, the creation of a modern political 'democracy' is striking. By 1925 Japan had achieved universal male suffrage and the electorate had increased from 400,000 in 1890 to 12 million (out of a total population of 63 million).

Among the most perceptive writers about Japan was the American historian Ruth Benedict, whose 1946 book *The Chrysanthemum and the*

Sword reflects the two sides of the Japanese character, the aesthetic and the militaristic. She wrote the book to try to prepare American officers for their occupation of Japan after 1945. Despite the pacifism which has characterized the country and the constitution since 1945, few Western observers doubt that the military side of the Japanese character still exists although it is not dominant today. Unlike Germany at the end of the Nazi period, the Japanese have rarely exhibited a sense of guilt. There are still political arguments about the re-writing of history textbooks used in Japanese schools to reflect the establishment view that Japan's advance into Manchuria in 1931 was justifiable and that atrocities in China and Korea were never actually committed.

All these historical factors are still relevant when we consider relations between Japan and its Asian neighbours – not only China, Korea and Taiwan, former areas of Japanese colonization – but also the Philippines, Singapore, Malaysia and Thailand, which were all occupied by Japanese forces between 1942 and 1945. It is true to say that the 'Greater East Asia Co-prosperity Sphere' (which Japan professed to be establishing during its drive for empire in the early 1940s) was nearly recreated in the 1980s (albeit in a purely economic rather than military sense) and that there is, therefore, a great deal of ambivalence on the part of those receiving Japanese investment, technology and trade today in these areas of Asia.

Japan's response to the West, therefore, also took the form of imitating Western imperialism and forming a colonial empire as Britain, France, Holland and even the United States had all done in other parts of Asia. In turn the response of the conquered Asian nations to the Japanese took the form of nationalism, particularly in the Philippines, Indonesia and Vietnam.

THE US IMPRINT ON ASIA SINCE 1945

Before 1850 East Asia was isolated. Its people were rigidly controlled under autocratic rule and generally not permitted to travel overseas, to trade, to vote or to have any kind of personal freedom, unlike their contemporaries in the Western world. Despite the ensuing century of Western contacts in Asia, it was only after 1945 and thanks to the Americans that Asians in general began to enjoy the benefits of free trade, freedom of movement, free press and freedom of religion. This is particularly true of Japan after 1945, and is also true of Taiwan and Korea – all three were occupied by US forces and deeply influenced by US culture. The American influence is less obviously present in the Chinese city states of Hong Kong and Singapore, which have had a British tradition. However, most of the privileged Chinese in these cities today are educated in American universities.

Asia owes an enormous debt to the United States, not only for the economic benefits of free trade and for providing a large consumer market for Asia's export products in the past thirty years, but also for the ideas of freedom that the Americans brought to the region. But Asian reality is always different from the appearance of things. The Asian view of democracy today is radically different from the American idea. For Asians, economic freedom comes before political freedom – they would rather have stability and consensus than an anarchic free press such as that of the Philippines. The Confucian ideas of respect, hierarchy and the moral integrity of rulers are more important than the democratic free-for-all which characterizes parliaments in London or Canberra, for example.

THAILAND

No other Asian country has handled its relations with the West so simply and successfully as Thailand or, under its old name, Siam. Much of this was due to the character of the two benevolent despots who ruled Siam during the whole of the second part of the nineteenth century, from 1851 to 1910. Mongkut (King Rama IV) was a Buddhist monk who was well read, both in the Pali Buddhist scriptures and also in Latin, mathematics, astronomy and English. He made all his leading subjects study English. He negotiated with Sir John Bowring in 1855 (entirely in English) a Treaty of Friendship and Commerce with Britain which contained more important concessions than Siam had ever granted before to a foreign power (and it was negotiated in less than one month). It limited the duty payable on goods imported by British merchants to 3% *ad valorem*, permitted the import of opium duty-free and laid down the scale of export duties. British subjects were to be permitted to purchase or rent land near the capital, Bangkok, and they were subject to the extraterritorial system by which jurisdiction over them was exercised by the British consul in Siam.

It is perhaps not an exaggeration to say that Siam owed to Mongkut (more than anyone else) the preservation of its independence when, by the end of the nineteenth century, all the other states of South-East Asia had come under European control. He could see clearly that if China had failed to maintain its isolation against European pressure, Siam must come to terms with threats from external forces and begin to accommodate itself to the new world in which Asian traditionalism appeared outworn and inefficient. Thus, he not only opened up Siam's trade with the outside world, he welcomed foreign residents and gave them extensive privileges. He brought in many Western advisers and was intensely interested in science and education. He promoted the building of canals, the construction of roads, shipbuilding, the teaching of foreign languages and he established a new coinage.

Mongkut's work was taken over by his son Chulalongkorn (King Rama V), who had been educated as a boy by Mrs Leonowens, the famous governess of *The King and I*. Chulalongkorn took his father's reforms one step further and established two English schools in Bangkok to which the aristocracy were forced to send their children. He abolished slavery and reformed the military system and taxation. The long-term results of these measures have been most striking, especially by contrast with Siam's two neighbours, French Indochina (now Vietnam) and Burma, ruled by the British. Siam's peasantry became a strong and independent class, free from the ancient serfdom, owning its own land, depositing money in the savings bank, in fact acquiring a stake in the country. This is still true today and it is a striking feature of the Thai character that the people are free, and independent capitalists. Chulalongkorn also encouraged the building of railways. He was able to fend off French encroachments on the border of Laos by playing off the British and the French against each other and becoming a buffer state between the two.

In all these fields – education, transport, finance, diplomacy – these two remarkable kings of Siam depended on European advisers. At the same time, just as in Thailand today, they used foreigners to modernize successfully without losing any of their traditional culture and confidence.

Thailand today is one of the most open countries for foreign investors, up to a point. The foreigner is encouraged to come and place his or her capital in Thailand in the freest possible way, as long as it is in the interests of Thailand. The long-term planning that has characterized the Thai civil service for decades was begun in the late nineteenth century under the reigns of Mongkut and Chulalongkorn. The monarchy has, in fact, been one of the key elements in Siam's, and now Thailand's, stability, confidence and successful response to the Western challenge.

KOREA

Before 1880 Korea was probably the most isolated country in the world, with virtually no external trade or outside contacts. Once a year a tributary mission was sent to Peking but the Qing Dynasty exercised little or no control, except in name, over the Korean peninsula. Korea was a small kingdom by Chinese, if not by European, standards. (The total population of the Korean peninsula today is just over 70 million, making it somewhat larger than England or France.) Korea's geographic problem is that it is at the point where three great empires – China, Japan and Russia – meet and conflict. This strategic location has meant that more often than not the peninsula has been divided over the course of the centuries. The present division between North and South Korea is complete and tragic in its human consequences.

In medieval times Korea was divided into the states of Koguryo, Paekche and Silla, which each exercised a dominant power at different times, with Japanese or Chinese influence playing a role. Even today there are many political differences within South Korea.

The last years of the Yi Dynasty (1392–1910) were characterized by the abrupt entry of foreign influences. The Japanese, playing the same role as the Americans in Japan in the 1850s, forced the opening of Korea in 1876. American influence was also present through the strong missionary effort. There was a brief decade of Chinese ascendancy from 1882 to 1894 but, after the victory of Japan in the Sino-Japanese War, the Japanese became the dominant power in Korea. The Russians meanwhile continued to expand into the Far East with the building of the Trans-Siberian railway in the 1890s, but their defeat by Japan in 1905 left Japan in a strong position, ruling Taiwan, dominating Korea and expanding in Manchuria. Despite the growth of a strong nationalist spirit in Korea, Japan annexed the country in August 1910 and Korea became a full Japanese colony. Although Japanese colonial rule lasted only for thirty-five years, or the span of a single generation, it had a profound and negative impact on the Korean economy and culture, suppressing nationalism and imposing the Japanese language and administration.

Korea, then, had the double misfortune of being geographically placed in the strategic 'cockpit' of North-East Asia between three great powers, and also, deeply influenced as it was by the Confucian culture of China and isolated from the outside world, being perhaps the least well prepared of the Asian nations to meet the Western challenge. During the last fifty years the country has suffered the set-back of becoming a Japanese colony, the devastation of the 1950–3 war, and the rule of the northern half of the peninsula by the most absolute Communist dictatorship. In this perspective the economic renaissance of South Korea since 1960 is all the more amazing. South Korea's finest hour was the staging of the 1988 Olympics in Seoul, which brought full international recognition of the country's achievements. Nevertheless, a lingering suspicion of foreigners remains from the centuries-old tradition of the 'hermit kingdom'.

South Korea remains a difficult country in which to do business and in which to invest. Nevertheless, the high proportion (around 25%) of the population who are Christian, and the country's strong links with the United States, do much to mitigate these characteristics. In the twenty-first century, the enigma of the future of the Korean peninsula remains. Contrary to all expectations, North Korea's totalitarian regime has survived the demise of the USSR and is supported by China. History suggests that the Korean peninsula will continue to be a battleground for influence, economic and political, between Russia, China, the USA and Japan.

INDONESIA

In 1292 the Polos, on their way home from China, visited Sumatra, stopping at the port of Perlak, where they found that the numerous Muslim traders had converted the natives to Islam. This was the first and most lasting foreign influence on the Indonesian archipelago, where today 88% of a population of about 238 million professes to be Muslim. The later arrival of the Portuguese (mainly in Timor) and then the Dutch had an important but less lasting influence. The Dutch ruled Indonesia from the time of the formation of the Dutch East India Company in 1602 until 1948. But it is surprising, considering this long period of colonial rule, how shallow the European influence has been on the culture. Economically, Indonesia has always been well endowed with natural resources, not only rich in its plantations but also, more recently, in the important discoveries of natural gas and oil. However, the need to provide for the large and dense population of Java has meant that per-capita income remains low even in the midst of plenty. During the period of Dutch colonial rule much of the wealth of Indonesia was drained off, finishing up in Amsterdam and The Hague. The fierce anti-colonial struggle of the aftermath of the Second World War left a bitter taste in Indonesia. It deprived the country of much-needed foreign capital for several decades. In the 1980s the attitude of the Indonesian ruling elite began to change with the arrival of a new, post-colonial generation in power. Today there is a much more relaxed acceptance of the need for foreign capital, foreign technology and management in Indonesia.

Much depends, for investors, on the transparency and honesty of the government in Jakarta (as in Manila): returns on capital have been consistently better under honest regimes, which do not add unnecessarily to the cost of doing business.

MALAYSIA AND SINGAPORE

Britain, or at least the East India Company, acquired Penang in 1786 for purely naval purposes. The architect of the future state of Singapore was Sir Stamford Raffles, who had been a successful Lieutenant-Governor of Java from 1810 to 1816 (during the Anglo-Dutch alliance following the Napoleonic War), where, among other things, he abolished slavery. His dream of making Batavia (now called Jakarta) the centre of a new British empire in the Indonesian islands failed, but on 28 January 1819 he founded the port of Singapore, which was to become the strategic port commanding the Malacca Straits, still today the funnel for the oil-tanker trade from the Gulf to East Asia. The Straits Settlements developed gradually during the nineteenth century, with the British generally leaving the local sultans in power while controlling overseas trade and maintaining naval supremacy.

As with the Dutch, the British influence in the Malay peninsula and in the British-ruled territories of Sarawak and North Borneo (the eastern portion of modern Malaysia) was neither very deep nor lasting. In all these scattered regions the British acquired an empire, in historian Sir John Seeley's apt phrase 'in a fit of absence of mind', and without any coherent purpose except for expanding trade and commerce. The original attraction of the East Indies had been that of the Spice Islands. The subsequent development of rubber plantations greatly accelerated the economic development of Malaya.

The British North Borneo Company concentrated mainly on timber concessions of teak and mahogany. But the difficulties of communication, transport and climate mitigated against any large or lasting European settlements.

THE PHILIPPINES

The Philippines is often regarded as a country with more affinity culturally and politically with Latin America than with Asia because of its Roman Catholic and Spanish characteristics. In fact, the underlying language and culture of the Philippines is not very different from the Bahasa Malay of Malaysia and the Indonesian islands. The Spanish influence on the Philippines began in the early 1500s and, with the annual visit of the Manila galleon bringing silver from Mexico, continued until 1898 when the American Commodore Dewey sunk the Spanish fleet in Manila Bay and the Philippines became the first American colony in Asia. Following the Proclamation of Filipino Independence by Emilio Aguinaldo, US foreign policy was somewhat divided and, while the Filipinos wanted independence, the Americans provided a colonial administration of a very different type from the European powers with a Washington-appointed Governor-General but a popularly elected senate and legislature in Manila. The United States had thus, by the 1930s and within a short period of time, introduced an advanced form of political democracy into the Philippines.

The impact of American political institutions was, however, as elsewhere in Asia, a fairly superficial one. The greatest and most beneficial impact of the American influence was the spread of education, as the spread of the Roman Catholic religion had been the greatest legacy of the Spanish. The economy meanwhile was tied to that of the United States and dependent on American largesse. This dependency has been a continuing characteristic, along with the presence of the American military bases (until the 1990s), which provided much employment and foreign currency. The Japanese occupation of the Philippines between 1941 and 1944 left some bitterness but also accelerated, as it did elsewhere in South-East Asia, the coming of independence in 1947. However, many economic problems remained and the Americans continued to dominate Filipino trade and investment. Political corruption has been a constant theme in the Philippine governments both before and since independence, culminating in the rule of Marcos in the 1980s. As in Indonesia, the Philippine stock market has had periods of buoyancy under capable and honest administration, followed by depressed years when corrupt politicians were in power. One interesting theme for the future is the wealth of natural resources in the Philippines, and China's growing appetite for copper and for oil, which used to be major constituents of the Manila market.

4

China's Foreign Policy

A new great power has arisen in the East with a quiet, patient, long-term strategy of securing its needs in terms of resources and raw materials by strategic planning and diplomatic forays into other emerging nations.

Despite the large rise in China's demand for raw materials in the past twenty years, its per-capita consumption of commodities is still very modest. Compared to the US, China's per-capita consumption of copper is less than one-third and aluminium less than one-fifth, so

Table 4.1: How much does one man consume? *Source: The Economist*

Consumption per capita based on 2004		US	Japan	China
Population	millions	293	127	1,300
Number of households	millions	110	48	365
Average number of persons per household	persons	2.7	2.6	3.6
Energy consumption (kg oil equivalent per head)	kgoe	8,750	4,457	998
Electricity consumption (kwh per head)	kwh	13,223	7,888	1,672
Petroleum consumption (gallons per day per person)	g/day/person	2.9	1.8	0.2
Daily calorie consumption (daily/pc)	cal. per capita	3,808	2,774	3,014
Consumer expenditure: Food, beverages & tobacco (US$) per capita	$/person	2,590	3,648	163
Fish consumption	kg per capita	22	65	27
Meat consumption	kg per capita	129	45	58
Personal computers	per capita	0.6	0.5	0.1
Television sets	per capita	0.9	0.7	0.4

looking ahead twenty years we can easily imagine that China may account for nearly 40% of global metal consumption.

China's strategy is comprised of several policies:

> **First**, become a major investor in natural-resource projects – China's oil companies have invested over US$40 billion in oil-exploration projects in Angola, Gabon, Algeria, Indonesia and Australia. CNOOC recently explored an US$18 billion takeover bid for the American oil company UNOCAL. China also announced a major investment in the Australian iron-ore industry with BHP, and a US$1 billion investment in a nickel mine in Papua New Guinea. In May 2005, a delegation from Alberta in the western part of Canada visited Beijing to secure Chinese interest in the huge oil-tar-sands deposits in their province.

> **Secondly**, China is now increasingly signing bilateral free-trade agreements with commodity-exporting countries such as South Africa, Chile and the Gulf States led by Saudi Arabia. When the

Table 4.2: China and global comparison – consumer durables (per 1,000 persons)

	Passenger Cars	2 Wheelers	TV Sets	Personal Computers	Mobile Phones
India	6	53	83	7	52
China	12	26	350	28	269
Brazil	64	28	349	75	263
France	491	40	632	347	647
Japan	428	106	785	382	637
Mexico	107	na	282	82	na
USA	480	15	938	658	488

Chart 4.3: Mobile phones – subscriber base (China and India)

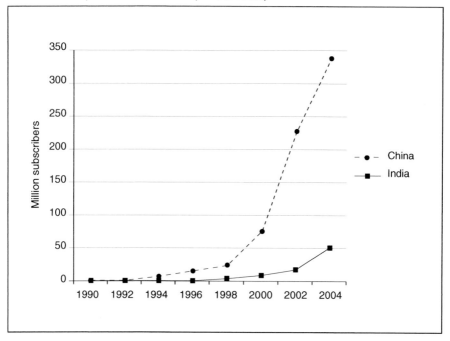

Chinese president Hu Jintao visited Latin America at the end of 2004, he announced US$8.5 billion of Chinese investment in Brazil's infrastructure and nearly US$20 billion in Argentina.

Thirdly, there is inevitably going to be pressure on China to secure its energy and raw-material needs via military means. If we reflect on the history of the last 200 years we see that Britain used its Royal Navy in the nineteenth century to secure the safety of its commercial interests around the world and the United States has used similar means, especially in the Middle East to secure oil supplies. China will have to keep building up its navy to protect shipping through the Malacca Straits from the Gulf and it will increasingly send military expeditions overseas, for example to Africa, to protect vital interests there. The real danger is that China might sell nuclear weapons or other high-technology weapons to its trading partners such as Iran, in return for oil supplies.

AFRICA

China sent more than 10,000 men to the Sudan to secure access to the rich oil and gas reserves in the southern part of the country, to build the pipelines and to provide some military security for these assets. In other parts of Africa, China is equally active, for example in Sierra

Table 4.4: China and India – forecast demand for commodities 2020 (million tonnes)

	2004 China and India	2020 China and India	2020 As a % of World Consumption
Steel	355	1,061	55.8
Aluminium	7	21	38.2
Nickel	0.2	0.5	21
Copper	4	11	34.8
Oil	378	1,086	16.1
Cement	942	1,629	44.7
Coal (oil eqvt.)	977	2,882	58.3
Iron ore	465	1,385	58.3
Bauxite	33	99	35.1
Cotton	9	26	56.8
Soy oil	9	28	46.2
Sugar	32	86	31.8

Table 4.5: China's imports from emerging markets

- **Food** – Thailand, Malaysia, Brazil, Argentina

- **Minerals** – Australia, Brazil, Chile, South Africa

- **Fuel** – Indonesia, Russia, Middle East, Africa

Leone, where since the end of the civil war in 2002 the only new foreign investors are Chinese. The main sectors they are interested in are fishing, textiles, sugar and tourism. Western diplomats suggest that the Chinese influx into West Africa could signal longer-term plans for settlements in Africa, which is a continent three times the size of China, with only two-thirds of the population. In a strange way this reflects the medieval fascination with Africa which the great Chinese voyages of exploration in 1421 fanned. (The Ming emperor was especially pleased to receive the first giraffe.)

THE MIDDLE EAST

The Chinese appear to be particularly interested in moving into areas which have been shunned by European and American companies. Iran is another major trading partner with US$4 billion of exports to China in 2004 (75% oil and gas). Chinese companies, like the big white-goods group Haier, have opened joint-venture factories in Isfahan, in the southern part of Iran, but the trade is mostly one-way. Over 50% of China's oil imports still come from the Middle East, 25% from Africa, so the diplomatic relationship with the Islamic world will grow in importance for China in the next twenty years.

LATIN AMERICA

Another area where there has been a flurry of diplomatic and commercial activity in 2004–5 is Latin America. This too is driven by Chinese hunger for strategic raw materials. China is now consuming 30% of world steel, iron-ore and tin production, and over 20% of world aluminium and zinc. The Chinese government attempted, through one of its proxy state-owned companies, to acquire a major nickel company in Canada recently, but there was a political outcry which may have postponed, if not cancelled the deal, so the Chinese are looking south to Brazil, Argentina, Peru and Chile. Latin American sales to China in 2004 grew nearly 50% to nearly US$22 billion. The main products are copper, iron ore and soy beans.

Unlike the Japanese companies in the 1980s which made small investments in the region, principally to establish 'listening posts' to monitor producers and competitors, China, by contrast, is intent on controlling assets and exerting political influence. China has for

Chart 4.6: Iron-ore imports to China in 2004 *Source: Mysteel*

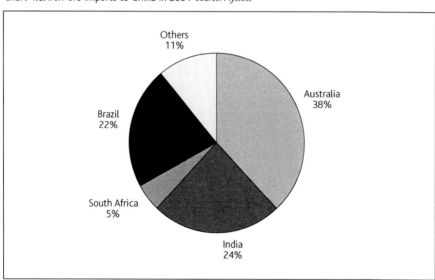

example two majority joint-venture projects in iron ore and aluminium with CVRD, the largest mining group in Brazil. It was clear from the visit of the Brazilian president to Beijing in 2004 that a major new strategic relationship has been formed. Many of the Latin American countries are happy to shake off the dominance of the United States, and welcome the Chinese interest in their continent. China does not neglect the smaller nations either – for example, Caribbean islands such as Grenada and Dominica because they have agreed to recognize China rather than Taiwan in exchange for sizeable aid packages (the same applies in Africa).

There are however some problems and obstacles. In Mexico, Guatemala, the Dominican Republic and Honduras there has been a sharp downturn since all US textile quotas were removed in January 2005. As already mentioned, the Chinese had within two months gone from 16% market share in the US textile market to over 60%, and this was mainly at the expense of these small Latin American countries.

Chart 4.7: Total coal imports to China *Source: China coal market network*

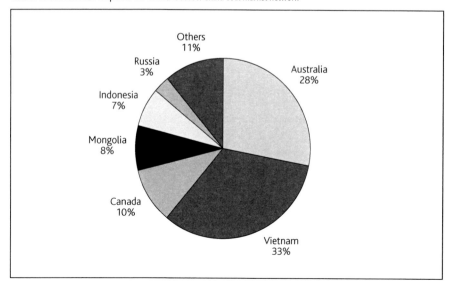

AUSTRALIA

China's good trade and diplomatic links with Australia are based on a mutually complementary relationship. Australia provides, for example, nearly 40% of China's iron ore, followed by India (24%) and Brazil (22%). The boom in infrastructure development and office and apartment building in Shanghai and Beijing has depended on these sources. China's needs will drive new investment in mining projects over the next decade, but, in the mean time, prices for these minerals will rise.

Table 4.8: Crude-oil imports by source (tonnes)

	2004	%
Saudi Arabia	17,244,382	14
Oman	16,347,755	13
Angola	16,208,232	13
Iran	13,237,341	11
Sudan	5,770,448	5
Vietnam	5,348,187	4
Yemen	4,912,284	4
Congo	4,773,270	4
Indonesia	3,428,621	3
Australia	1,510,298	1
Iraq	1,306,475	1
Kuwait	1,253,961	1
Qatar	142,395	0
Others	31,331,860	26
Total	**122,815,510**	100

Australia also provides nearly a third of China's coal needs; only Vietnam surpasses it, with the unique geographical advantage of being on China's southern border, positioned to supply the rapidly industrializing south-eastern region centred on Guangdong. Most of China's coal reserves are in the north-east near Mongolia, which itself has large coal, copper and gold reserves with which to supply China.

OIL

It is interesting to study the list of sources from which China obtains its crude oil, of which it will have a growing need in the next two decades. In addition to the obvious OPEC producers – Saudi Arabia, Kuwait and Iran – Africa is well represented, especially Angola, Sudan (where, remember, China maintains 10,000 men either operating, building or guarding the oil fields and oil pipelines) and Congo,

Table 4.9: China's search for oil and gas

- **Xinjiang (Tarim Basin)**
- **Offshore – South China Sea**
    - **– Daoyu (Senkaku) Islands**
- **L.N.G.   – Indonesia**
    - **– Australia**
- **Africa (Sudan)**
- **Middle East and Central Asia**

whose supply has grown tenfold in five years. Vietnam has also become an important supplier of raw materials, including oil, as have Indonesia and Australia.

China will seek to diversify and secure its energy needs as much as possible, by forging diplomatic and if necessary military links with friendly oil-producing nations. To repeat: in this way, China is acting no differently to other great powers such as Britain and the United States in the Middle East over the past century.

RELATIONSHIPS AND RISKS IN THE CHINESE SPHERE OF INFLUENCE

Taiwan

No single issue is as important, for an investor in Hong Kong, China and Taiwan today and in the next ten years, as how China will manage to integrate Taiwan. Since the civil war ended in 1949 and Chiang Kai Shek left the mainland with nearly a million followers to cross over to the former Japanese colony, of Formosa, there has been a stalemate between the 'two Chinas'. Paradoxically, both sides accepted that there was only 'one China'. Chiang Kai Shek set up a national parliament in Taipei where there were representatives from every Chinese province.

The Communist leaders in Beijing regarded Taiwan as a renegade province that was temporarily lost to the mainland but would be regained in due course. The military option for China to invade Taiwan was not however easy to exercise because the US lent its support to Chiang and the Taiwanese for most of the post-war period; with some US economic as well as military aid, Taiwan rapidly became an industrial and technological powerhouse, with strong links to Silicon Valley.

In 1987 Chiang's son Chiang Chingkuo surprised the world by moving from what had been effectively a military dictatorship, towards fully democratic elections. Within ten years Chang's old party, the Kuomintang, had ceded control of Taiwan's presidency and parliament to the islanders' party, the Democratic Progressive Party (DPP). Suddenly China's policy of patient diplomacy, backed by the never cancelled option of military action, became less effective in the face of a possible declaration of independence by President Chen Shuiban of Taiwan.

In 2005 the Chinese leaders took the initiative by inviting the opposition leaders of Taiwan to visit the mainland, and so a historian could enjoy the spectacle of the leaders of the Chinese Communist Party and the Kuomintang shaking hands in Nanjing (former capital of Nationalist China and Sun Yat Sen's shrine) for the first time since their civil war ended fifty-six years earlier. China was apparently willing to offer Taiwan almost every kind of autonomy – that it could keep its own flag, its own army, its own political parties, its own free democratic and capitalist system – if it would only agree that it was part of one China.

I asked Ambassador Wu Jianmin, President of the Foreign Affairs School for Chinese diplomats, if that meant a federal solution. He replied no, it was more similar to the Hong Kong solution of 'one country, two systems'. Although China had reasserted its sovereignty over Hong Kong in June 1997, it had allowed Hong Kong to maintain its free economic system (but not democracy) for a further fifty years, until 2047, by which time, as Deng Xiaoping predicted, there would be little difference between the two systems on either side of the border. (This was already becoming true less than ten years after the Chinese handover.)

With Taiwan therefore, China appeared to be very confident that it could win its objective in a peaceful manner and also very patient, such that it would also extend Taiwan at least fifty years before it was fully integrated into the 'motherland'.

At the same time China left no doubt that if Taiwan did not agree to talk, and compromise on China's proposals, it would maintain the option of a military invasion. The US defence secretary pointed out in 2005 that China's military spending had grown far more rapidly than was necessary for its own defence and that the build-up of both the Chinese navy and airforce could only be aimed at one target – that is, a cross-straits invasion of Taiwan. This remains the biggest single risk to investors in the region.

Hong Kong would be caught up in the middle of a new Chinese civil war and would suffer a drastic fall in trade and confidence. Some observers think that China could actually achieve a rapid 'decapitation' of Taiwan's government and install a friendly regime without loss of life or economic damage, but although the risk of a China–Taiwan confrontation remains, the probability is probably less than 10%. In the mean time the economic links between the two Chinese communities become rapidly stronger every year.

In *The 2024 Report*, Norman Macrae predicted in 1984 that when the world searches for a new model for economic development in the early twenty-first century the global competition will be won by an elderly Taiwanese professor who recommends the economic model of Taiwan, i.e. minimum government interference, low taxes, few regulations, and rapid two-year product changes by small family-run companies. Indeed, judged by results, Taiwan has the world's most successful economy; with a population of 20 million, over a thirty-year period, it has averaged 8–10% economic growth every year. The Taiwanese model has already been adopted by many of the Chinese corporations situated along the coast, especially in Guangdong Province. The speed with which world export markets change today demands the kind of flexibility which is built into these small, family-run or municipal companies or 'SMSE' (small and medium-sized enterprises).

There are over one million Taiwanese living in China, about 500,000 in Shanghai alone. There are thousands of Taiwanese-owned factories in Guandong and Fujian provinces, as well as in Shanghai. Taiwan's input, not only of capital and marketing know-how, but also of technology, is enormously important to China's modernization. There is no doubt that the combination of the two Chinas is and will be a formidable economic super-power. The alternative is unthinkable to the pragmatic and economy-oriented Chinese mind. The uncertainty however may continue for many years to come.

Table 4.10: Greater China *Source: United Nations, Central Intelligence Agency*

Country	Population (mn) 2004	GDP by Expenditure (USD Bn) 2003
China	1,299.0	1,409
Taiwan	22.7	282
Hong Kong	6.9	159
Macau	0.5	8

From the US standpoint however it was felt that there was a danger in 2005–8 of Taiwan's president feeling under pressure and announcing a new constitution with a move towards independence. In the eyes of the US and of Japan, reunification of China and Taiwan might make China too strong, and specifically it would give China control of the strategic Taiwan straits, on which Japan depends for its trade and oil imports. The US policy is therefore to restrain President Chen from any rash declaration of independence and instead to move towards a loose 'confederation' whereby Taiwan keeps much of its autonomy. 2008 will be a key date with the next presidential elections in Taiwan, the Olympic Games in Beijing, and a new president in the United States.

As one experienced commentator said about China, 'They can wait for ever'; China is so confident about its own economic and military development as a great power, they can accept anything from Taiwan, except independence.

Hong Kong

Hong Kong has begun to prosper again under Chinese sovereignty, after about six years of economic depression following the 1997 handover and right up to the outbreak of SARS in early 2003. China evidently decided to support Hong Kong's economy by liberalizing the cross-border trade and maintaining Hong Kong's role as the international financial centre for China. Ambassador Wu also said that Hong Kong has a very important role to play in the regional economic and monetary integration which he expects to develop over the next ten years. 'In Asia', he said, 'we need a common currency and an expanded monetary union similar to the Euro.' Hong Kong might be China's preferred centre for the central bank of such an Asian currency.

The Chinese, being very pragmatic, realize that Hong Kong has a long history and tradition of free economic and financial development and a unique population of expatriate experts in law, finance, accounting, shipping and insurance. This is Hong Kong's asset, which protects its unique status in the decades ahead.

The Hong Kong view is that China does not understand Hong Kong, which needs a democratically elected chief executive and an accountable government. Decision-making under Chief Executive Tung Chee Wa was paralysed by the need to consult Beijing. The new chief executive in 2005 is Sir Donald Tsang, whose background as a civil servant may help him to develop more effective long-term policy-making. Hong Kong's total dependence on China is not healthy and the government has lost its sense of direction. With the new competition from Shanghai and possibly Beijing, Hong Kong is no longer the most vibrant and dynamic financial centre that it was in the past.

China's Wild West

Many Chinese dynasties prior to the present Communist government, dreamed of populating and developing the vast open spaces in the west of China in the provinces of Sinkiang, Tibet and Inner Mongolia. Since 1949 several million Han Chinese have been sent, willingly or unwillingly, to settle in Tibet and in the western areas where the minority tribes, mainly Uighurs, predominate.

There are an estimated 70 million Muslims in China today, mainly in this area, which borders with the new Muslim states born out of the Soviet Union since 1991 – Kazakhstan, Uzbekistan, Tajikistan and Kyrgyzstan. Unrest in these Muslim countries can easily spill over into China's Muslim population. After September 2001, China used the excuse of cracking down on Muslim terrorists to exercise a much tighter control over its western and Muslim population.

The added economic incentive for this policy was the discovery in the Tarim Basin of a vast oil reserve which is expected to start producing by 2008–10. Although it is nearly 3,000 miles from the sea and therefore very expensive to pump along enormous pipelines, China's oil dependence today is such that they care less about the economic cost of production than of the need to be more self-sufficient. Most of the western areas of Sinkiang are under the control of the Chinese military, but this area will be very important to watch and monitor carefully over the next twenty years. If Beijing's control weakened there would be a risk of secession and civil war in this region.

North Korea

North Korea, with a common border of almost a thousand miles with China, remains an unpredictable and dangerous element in the strategic power game in North Asia. In 2005 China was supplying 80% of North Korea's food and fuel needs, and even that was insufficient as the evidence of many starving North Koreans proved. The regime of Kim Jong Il was not easy to control, even by their closest ally. I was told by senior Chinese officials in Beijing that the Chinese ambassador in Pyongyang could not travel far from his Embassy and certainly not freely around the country.

The six-party talks involving the US, Russia, China, North Korea, South Korea and Japan did not progress very far in the face of intransigence from the North Koreans, who insisted on maintaining their nuclear research. China clearly told them not to develop a nuclear weapon. For one of the major risks of this development would be that Japan would feel the need to go nuclear. China itself would be threatened by having a nuclear neighbour so close. China claimed that the supply of oil and food to North Korea was essentially humanitarian and that they did not want to prop up an unsavoury regime. There is also a domestic angle to this in that there are very large Korean minorities in the Manchurian area adjacent to North Korea who might become restive if the North Korean economy or regime collapsed.

The unpalatable truth is, that, apart from the Korean people themselves, none of the great powers really want to see a re-united peninsula: and even the Seoul government admits that they could not afford the reconstruction costs (at least not on the German model).

Table 4.11: Economic potential of a unified Korea *Source: United Nations*

	South Korea	North Korea
Population (millions)	49	23
GDP by expenditure (USD Bn) 2003	528	11
GDP per capita (USD) 2003 Actual	11,058	494
Resources	Industries: electronics, telecommunications, automobile production, chemicals, shipbuilding, steel	Industries: military products, machine building, electric power, chemicals, mining (coal, iron ore, magnesite, graphite, copper, zinc, lead, and precious metals)
	Agriculture – Products: rice, root crops, barley, vegetables, fruit, cattle, pigs, chickens, milk, eggs, fish	Agriculture – Products: rice, corn, potatoes, soybeans, pulses, cattle, pork, eggs
	Exports – Commodities: Semiconductors, wireless telecommunications equipment, motor vehicles, computers, steel, ships, petrochemicals	Exports – Commodities: minerals, metallurgical products, manufactures (including armaments), textiles, fishery products

Japan

In both the case of Taiwan and China and with North Korea, perception and reality are very different. The West, and particularly the United States, perceives the danger of war or nuclear proliferation. In the East, there is generally a more relaxed approach and a patient long-term view. Much more dangerous in the long term is the possibility of a confrontation with Japan.

The modern relationship between China and Japan goes back deep into history. Japan owes nearly all its culture to China. The Kanji system of writing comes from Chinese ideograms. Buddhism came via China, from India to Japan. The city of Kyoto was laid out to the same pattern as the ancient Chinese capital of Chang'an (today called Xian). The Emperor of Japan today lives in a fortified palace in the heart of Tokyo which is not dissimilar to the Forbidden City in Beijing.

This relationship of 'older brother and younger brother' changed dramatically after Japan's modernization under the Meiji restoration in the 1860s. By 1895 Japan's military power was such that it was able to defeat China decisively and take over Taiwan, which it held as a Japanese colony for fifty years, and also invade the whole of Korea as well as Manchuria. In the treaty of Shimonoseki Japan gained all the commercial privileges that the Western powers had in China.

In 1905 Japan defeated the Russians and took more land in Manchuria. The anti-Japanese riots in China in the spring of 2005 were based on the outrage that the Chinese people felt at Japan's history textbooks which deliberately excluded the truth about the Sino-Japanese war of 1931–45, especially the Rape of Nanjing and other Japanese atrocities. The Japanese held down almost one-third of China during the 1940s and they were not welcomed back as investors and businessmen very rapidly.

The real tectonic shift in Asia since 1990 has been China's awakening and assumption of economic leadership. Fifteen years ago Japan still led Asia, but today China is the leader, both economically and politically. A recent Japanese report highlighted the fact that China had just become the third-largest exporting nation after the US and Japan, which it will soon overtake. By 2010 China will surpass Japan to become the world's second-largest car manufacturer. By 2010 China is also expected to account for 22% of the global electronics market. In consumer electronics China will overwhelm Japan in terms of production. Although these forecasts may not turn out to be precisely accurate in terms of time frame, it is hard to argue with the overall trend, particularly given the shrinking and ageing Japanese population.

China and Japan today have a mutual interest in building trade and investment but the weight of history is still stronger. China sent a nuclear-powered submarine into the disputed area of the Daoyu (or Senkaku) Islands where there are reputed to be large oil and gas fields. This was a shock to the Japanese, who have begun to rearm and modernize their navy to respond to this threat. There are therefore real dangers that tension based on historical enmities could escalate into some kind of conflict.

Indeed, a June 2005 report said that Japan's younger generation of lawmakers in the Diet – in their forties and fifties – are much more assertive about their national sovereignty and willing to rearm and send naval forces to protect Japanese drilling efforts in the Senkaku Islands. In addition, these younger members of the Diet have ended Japan's aid to China (itself a kind of war-reparations payment).

Japan's economy is still three times larger than China's, but it has an ageing population and an uncompetitive industrial base. Not only is Japan afraid of China in an economic, but also in a military, sense. The Sino-Japanese relationship is enormously complicated by their joint history and even today young Chinese are brought up to hate the Japanese because of the atrocities committed during the 1931–45 war.

Chinese government officials said that boycotting Japanese goods in China was not productive as there were over 30,000 Sino-Japanese joint ventures operating in China, over US$66 billion of Japanese investment in China, and possibly more than 10 million Chinese jobs depending on Japanese companies. Many of the cars in China are Japanese, especially Honda and Toyota. China and Japan need each other: one has the technology and the advanced industrial base, the other has the low-cost labour, the land, the young population and the growing consumer market of the future. Nevertheless, it is certain that during the next twenty years, there will be continued friction and possible clashes between these two Asian giants.

One area where they may come into conflict has already been noted: in the search for oil and gas, in the disputed islands, called the Daoyu Islands by the Chinese and the Senkaku Islands by the Japanese – uninhabited rocks in the China Sea north of Taiwan but claimed by the Japanese since 1895. The Chinese leadership often refers back to maps of the Chinese Empire made by the Ching Dynasty in the 1700s and early 1800s. In the South China Sea, they also have disputes about the Paracel Islands and the Spratlys with both Vietnam, Indonesia and the Philippines. Here too is the possibility of large offshore oil reserves but China seems to have decided to co-operate and share these reserves with their Asian neighbours, in what Ambassador Wu refers to as a 'win-win' policy of co-operation to develop natural resources. In the case of Japan they are not so willing to co-operate.

Japan will probably amend its constitution, which has since 1952 prohibited it from becoming a military power. This would enable Japan to rearm and its defence spending to exceed 1% of GNP. Japan will become 'a normal country again', sixty years after the end of the Second World War.

Foreign Trade and Diplomacy
Through most of its long history China has been a self-contained country – the 'Middle Kingdom' – which had little need for or curiosity about other countries. The last twenty-five years have brought rapid modernization and opening-up of China to foreign trade and investment. The result is that in 2005 China's foreign trade accounts for 50% of its GNP. Not only is China a major exporter of manufactured products, but it is also becoming a major buyer of commodities and natural resources as well as Western products and services.

China's greatest challenge in the next two decades will be how to behave as an international economic power. It is not easy for China's present government to evolve the necessary communication skills in international diplomacy, to rise to the challenge of becoming not just the leader in the Asian region, but a great power in the world.

Although China's rise is peaceful, many people around the world are uneasy about the growth and the size of China's economy and its new power. In particular, the United States is unsure of how to deal with the only other global power that can challenge American leadership. History shows that rising powers, like Japan and Germany in the early twentieth century, encounter problems.

The Chinese official government line is that China does not seek hegemony or world leadership and does not seek to dominate other nations. In the quest for natural resources it seeks to co-operate with other countries in win-win situations.

In Europe today, Ambassador Wu Jianmin hears from French businessmen and diplomats that 'China has become so strong, but you are taking away our jobs'; and even in Africa, in Tunisia, where the main export is textiles, the Tunisian prime minister commented that 'we admire your country, because China is a model of how to manage a large developing country, but on the other hand we are afraid of you'.

So there is a real danger of a protectionist backlash both in the West and in many developing countries against the growing trade of Chinese products. Despite China's early commitment to the World Trade Organization and its trading rules, the rapid rise of China's textile exports after the final removal of all textile quotas on 1 January 2005, has already made an alarming impact. China's share of the US textile market was estimated to have grown in two months from 16% to over 60%. Chinese competition shows signs of devastating many Third World textile exporters, especially in Africa and Central America.

China's quest for economic security is now the driving consideration of its foreign policy. It will try everything possible to develop internal sources of power: hydro-electric power from The Three Gorges Dam on the Yangtze River, nuclear power and oil from the Western Tarim Basin. But where internal sources are inadequate, it will also spare no effort to secure the raw materials its economy needs in every part of the globe. In recent years, for example, the Chinese have been stockpiling many key strategic metals from other countries, including copper and cobalt from Zambia and the Democratic Republic of the Congo.

5

A Forecast for the Year 2020

In the first edition of this book, written in 1991, I attempted to make a forecast for the year 2000. The main element of this forecast was that the world trading system would coalesce into three major economic blocs: Europe, East Asia and North America; this was based on the development of NAFTA, the United States, Canada and Mexico forming a free-trade zone; in addition, the European Economic Community or EU was developing from six original countries to a total of twenty-five countries with a population of nearly 500 million and forming a large economic area.

As for East Asia, it seemed likely, fifteen years ago, that Japan would dominate the free-trade area which was beginning to take shape, although the timetable for Asia's 'common market' was far behind that of North America and Europe. Today it is clear that China will be the dominant player in the Asian region and that, as has been discussed, the formation of a 'Greater China' confederation of China, Taiwan, Hong Kong and Macau would have very important economic and diplomatic consequences. There have been very important steps towards creating a free-trade area, for example between ASEAN – which consists of Malaysia, Singapore, Thailand, Indonesia, the Philippines, Brunei, Vietnam, Laos, Cambodia and Myanmar – and China.

Whereas fifteen years ago Japan was the main source of investment and lending to the South-East Asian countries, today China has become a major new trading partner buying raw materials and commodities and selling manufactured goods, mostly cheap consumer products such as motor bicycles, sewing machines and consumer electronics. By contrast with Europe, Asia is a free-trade, low-tariff, low-labour-cost area with little or nothing in the way of welfare spending and support. This means that for a global manufacturer looking to produce consumer goods with the maximum flexibility, it is much more attractive to base a factory in Asia, where labour can be hired cheaply and easily and there are fewer regulations.

Chart 5.1: Asia's move upmarket

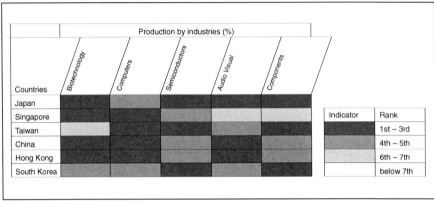

In 1990, the lowest-cost producers were Thailand and Hong Kong, today, India, Indonesia and China dominate the production of textiles, toys and shoes. Coming up behind are Vietnam, Pakistan and Bangladesh. Thailand is now a middle-income country that is focusing on higher-value-added products such as auto parts. If we focus on the disparity in factory wages the surprise is how quickly China has moved up the table from an average of US$35 a month in 1990 to perhaps US$160. Per-capita income in many of the major cities – Shanghai, Beijing and Guangzhou – is rapidly approaching that of Hong Kong.

CHINA'S CAPITAL MARKET

In December 1990, I was present for the re-opening of the Shanghai stock exchange for the first time since the Communist revolution in 1949. Although there were only two listed securities (both government bonds) and the ceremony took place in a rather dusty hall overlooked by the Russian consulate on the Soo Chow Creek at the end of the Bund, there was nevertheless an air of great excitement and expectation. Several elderly gentlemen, dressed incongruously in French berets, made an appearance and it transpired that they had been stockbrokers forty years earlier during the Nationalist period in China.

The day following the opening I gave a talk to the Chinese officials involved with the stock exchange, who asked me what was required for international pension funds and fund managers like ourselves to invest in China. I replied that the most important thing was to have a number of 'blue chip' companies which every international fund would have to own. When questioned, what were blue chips? I said IBM and Coca-Cola in the US, but in China it was more difficult to identify the leading names in 1990. The only brand which was well known to all of us in Hong Kong was Tsing Tao Beer, so I suggested that, and two years later in 1992 among the first four Chinese

Table 5.2: Average monthly factory wages   *Source: The Economist and ABN AMRO Research*

Country	1990 USD	2004* USD
Germany	3,520	5,680
US	2,225	3,664
UK	2,032	3,600
Italy	2,832	3,504
Australia	1,750	3,360
Japan	2,440	3,360
Singapore	485	1,600
South Korea	655	1,504
Hong Kong	590	912
Taiwan	700	896
South China (SEZs)	110	322
Malaysia	275	288
Thailand	120	192
China	35	160
India	60	128
Philippines	92	112
Sri Lanka	40	80
Indonesia	45	48

*based on 40-hour week

companies listed on the Hong Kong stock exchange as 'H' shares was indeed Tsing Tao Beer.

These early listings were not successful and the Chinese companies did not really know how to deal with foreign investors, provide proper annual accounts and communicate with their shareholders. There was however a rapid learning curve and by the late 1990s China already had a thousand companies listed on the Shanghai stock exchange: these came from all the provinces of China, including Tibet and Inner Mongolia, and from every sector of industry, from iron and steel to milk and bread. In the mean time, many of the top Chinese companies skipped Shanghai and its sister exchange in southern China, Shenzen, altogether to go straight for listings in Hong Kong

Table 5.3: Stock market capitalization as percentage of GDP

	Market Cap	GDP	%
China	522	1,353	38.6
Brazil	234	488	48.0
India	221	628	35.2
South Korea	294	605	48.6
Malaysia	250	103	242.7
Mexico	122	626	19.5
Russia	183	433	42.3
South Africa	267	160	166.9
Taiwan	379	286	132.5
Thailand	118	143	82.5
Turkey	68	239	28.5

mainly, but also in Singapore, London and New York. The biggest companies were the telecom giants, China Telecom, China Mobile and Unicom. Soon after that came the banks, led by the Bank of China and the four other big Chinese Banks – Bank of Communications, China Construction Bank, ICBC and Agricultural Bank of China, which are expected to be listed in 2005–7, before the opening, according to the WTO timetable, of the banking market in China in 2007 to foreign banks and insurance companies.

The Chinese approach to capital markets may be usefully contrasted to Russia. In 1991 the Soviet Communist Party lost power to the populist revolution under Boris Yeltsin. Soon afterwards they decided to privatize every state-owned enterprise through a system of giving vouchers to the entire population of 150 million Russians. Entrepreneurs quickly spotted the opportunity and bought up a vast majority of these vouchers into funds and achieved control of major Russian corporations, especially the oil and gas companies, which were the most valuable because they had an internationally traded commodity. Soon the 'Oligarchs' – Berezovsky, Abramovich, Friedman and Khordokovsky – became billionaires known in Russia and abroad for their control of the major Russian energy companies and banks. The government had entirely given up control and shareholdings in these major enterprises, with the exception of Gazprom. Belatedly, under President Putin, the Russian government, by 2005, was trying to regain control over what they considered to be some nationally strategic assets.

After Tiananmen Square in June 1989, the Chinese government was going to take no risks of losing control politically or socially, and certainly not financially. The Asian crisis of 1997–8 reinforced this fear of foreign speculators and capitalists who might destabilize China's currency or capital markets. Hence the early hopes for China's stock market were somewhat dimmed by the slow pace of reform. Although there were a thousand companies listed and nearly US$500 billion of theoretical market value available, the government controlled on average about 60% of these companies and one result was that there was little change in corporate governance or responsibility.

Although there were a handful of successful Chinese companies which had been started by entrepreneurs, such as Legend (later Lenovo) computer company, the vast majority of Chinese listed companies tend to be state-owned enterprises (SOEs). The result was that for five years, between 2000 and 2005, the Chinese economy continued to grow at nearly 10% per annum, (in other words it added 50% in terms of economic output and industrial production); while at the same time the Shanghai stock-exchange index declined by 50%. The result was many angry and disappointed Chinese investors.

The reasons for this disappointing performance were not hard to discover. The overhang of state-owned shares and the unwillingness of the Chinese government to relinquish control of major enterprises and allow them to act in a truly capitalist and market-oriented way had completely destroyed the spirit of the capital market, which depends everywhere on what J. M. Keynes called 'animal spirits' – the fast growth of private enterprises, the rapid wealth creation of private business, the cut and thrust of merger and acquisition, and competition in the market place.

Although it is estimated that 60% of China's exports and of its manufacturing output came from private enterprises (very often small and medium-sized enterprises belonging to local municipalities as well as foreign-owned companies), this was not reflected on China's stock exchanges. There may be, in the end, a link between Communist control of the 'commanding heights' of the economy and the performance of the stock exchange. There is also a link between the non-convertibility of the Chinese renminbi and the inability of foreign investors to gain access to Chinese 'A' shares.

In 2004–5 the Chinese government, emulating the model of Taiwan, opened their 'A' shares in a limited way through QFIIs (Qualified Foreign Institutional Investors), which were mainly Western banks and pension funds with over US$10 billion of assets. As in Taiwan the money would be locked up for a period of at least one year so that short-term speculation was barred.

Any visitor to Shanghai's magnificent modern stock exchange in the Pudong District today would be impressed by the ambition and scale of China's experiment with capital markets. It is often observed that the 'hardware' is all splendid and modern, but the 'software', i.e. the human capital and entrepreneurial freedom, is still missing. No one can doubt however that during the next twenty years all these elements will fall into place and that China will become a major destination for Western fund managers and institutional investors. The mere size of its existing market, US$500 billion (plus the Chinese companies listed in Hong Kong), would suggest that the global index funds will take a major stake in this market when it opens after 2007. If we look at the GNP and manufacturing output of China today, we may expect that the value of China's stock market will exceed 50% of GNP and it has therefore some room to grow and develop over the next five years.

Chart 5.4: Foreign direct investment in China 1990–2005

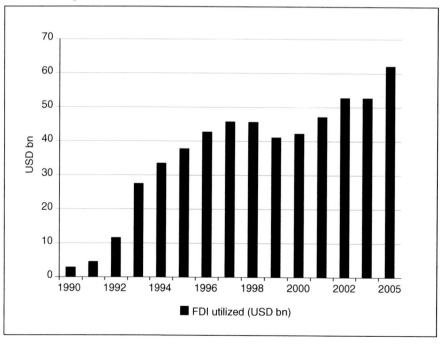

THE INFLUENCE OF THE OVERSEAS CHINESE

In the chart on the Chinese diaspora, we estimated that there were over 65 million overseas Chinese, the majority of whom live in Taiwan, Hong Kong, Singapore and other Asian countries where they are a minority. These communities have had a major impact in terms of trade and investment with China since it opened up in the early 1980s. They will continue to have a great influence, because of their financial and economic network, on how China develops and gains market share and global trade influence in the future. It is especially significant to monitor the movement of people and capital among the minority Chinese communities in Indonesia, Malaysia, and the Philippines, where political uncertainty and sometimes anti-Chinese feeling have caused emigration and capital flight.

It is however in the overseas Chinese communities in Australia, Canada, the United States and Europe, especially the UK, where we can see the most significant changes. Many of the Chinese students who went overseas to study, under Deng Xiaoping in the 1980s, have stayed overseas, but more than half have become 'returnees', sometimes with US passports, who are back in China and are the new wave of entrepreneurs and US-trained managers who are making China such an interesting new market. China has been intelligently enticing back these gifted and trained overseas Chinese (just as they have enticed back over a million Taiwanese into Shanghai and other business centres), because China desperately needs the management and technology know-how that these people can bring with them. Among the younger generation of the Chinese-American community too, there is a strong magnetic pull back to China not only to explore their roots but to exploit the business opportunities that China presents, particularly to someone speaking fluent Mandarin and understanding the local culture. It is also true that many of the foreign-born Chinese find the local culture quite different and intimidating if they have been born and educated in the West. Nevertheless, as we try to make intelligent forecasts about China in the next twenty years it is important to focus on this pool of talent which lies outside China but which China can use for its own modernization and rapid catch-up in science and technology. The business opportunity works both ways in the sense that the overseas Chinese invest in China and China gains access to Western markets through this important link.

In the 1992 edition of *The East–West Pendulum* I also focused on the Chinese communities in Vancouver and the appointment of Dr. David Lam as Lieutenant-Governor in the late 1980s. Vancouver remains an important location for wealthier retired Chinese immigrants from Hong Kong and elsewhere, but it is not such a dynamic business community today. After the handover of Hong Kong to China in 1997, one effect which had been little anticipated was that many Chinese who had obtained Canadian passports returned to Hong Kong and to China because the business opportunities and tax breaks were considerably more attractive in the East.

In Australia, too, there is a growing Chinese community that is deeply involved in the two way China–Australia trade, which has been booming in the past ten years. It is not an exaggeration to say that the Australian economy has benefited more than any other in the past five years from China's new demand for natural resources, for oil and gas, for minerals, for wool and other agricultural commodities and for some of the medical and service industries, which Australia has been able to provide. There is a naturally complementary relationship between the large and relatively under-populated continent of Australia, with its great natural resources, and China's vast population, with growing personal incomes, and shortage of strategic materials. Travel and tourism from China will also benefit Australia as it will Hong Kong, Macau and Singapore.

San Francisco, or the 'Golden Mountain' as the Chinese have called it since the Gold Rush of 1849, remains an important and long-established Chinese community, with great collections of Chinese art and antiques. The US–China trade is now largely focused on the West Coast, with Los Angeles also being an important port for China's growing imports. Given modern technology and communications, the US–China relationship is less focused on any particular city or state and concerns, at the time of writing in 2005, are really about possible US protectionist measures; against the sudden jump in Chinese textile imports, for instance; and also Chinese reluctance to give in to US pressure to revalue their currency against the dollar.

With China's fast-growing foreign-exchange reserves of over US$ 600 billion being largely invested in US treasury bonds, there is also a complementary relationship between China's export strength and American financing needs. The Chinese community in the USA will also play an important role in the trade and investment links that so many US companies have with China today. Although there may be short-term disputes and tensions, there is no doubt that over the long run China and America need each other, both as markets and as capital providers and that the links – economic, financial and even educational – will grow stronger every year.

Finally, in the United Kingdom there is a growing Chinese community, mainly based in London and in the Midlands. Unlike

Table 5.5: Tourism in China 2000–2020

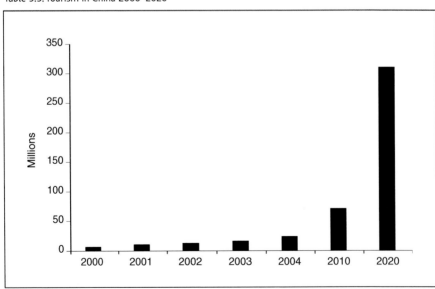

some of the other immigrant communities which have caused political tensions and difficulties, the Chinese have been almost universally welcomed as hard-working contributors to the national economy. The number of Chinese students in British universities continues to climb steadily, particularly as they are willing to pay full fees in some UK universities that have funding difficulties. Since the Hong Kong handover there is a fairly large community of Hong Kong Chinese people with UK passports who often feel equally at home in London or Hong Kong.

Not only in the UK but throughout Europe the Chinese influence is steadily growing. In Berlin, for example, the most fashionable club is now the China Club and there is a large Chinese business community based there with links not only to Germany but to Eastern Europe. So the economic dynamism of China and of the Chinese communities of Asia continues to ripple out in a myriad of ways throughout the Western world.

It has been argued that the overseas Chinese are not, in fact, as successful at managing large, structured corporations as the Japanese and the Koreans. Typically the most successful Chinese businesses have been small, family firms. There is an inherent problem in the change of generations – very often the sons, though better educated than their fathers, do not have the same hunger and drive, and the growth rate of the company slows down. This phenomenon is familiar to experienced investors in South-East Asia. However, more and more Chinese family companies are hiring professional managers in order to maintain the company's dynamism beyond the first generation.

DEMOGRAPHICS

Although I have tried to demonstrate the broad influence and economic power of the community of 65 million Chinese people living outside China, it is to China itself that we must return to understand the future influence of the East. In economic terms the

65 million of the Chinese diaspora have for the moment much more impact than the 1.3 billion people on the mainland but the challenge of that vast number remains.

One of the leading ideas in the 1992 edition of *The East–West Pendulum* was the view espoused by a leading British statesman in 1936 that 'sheer biological and geographical facts would change the balance of the world by 2100'. With the industrialization of Russia, India and China there would be a change in the balance of world power. In the fifteen years since I wrote the first edition, this change has become ever more visible. The developed countries (the USA, Europe and Japan) have gone from 33% of the world's population in 1950 to 18% in 2005 and they will be 12% in 2050.

The developing countries, by that time, will constitute close to 90% of world population. For example, the major Islamic countries (Indonesia, Pakistan, Bangladesh, Egypt, Iran, Syria, Yemen, Turkey, Iraq, Saudi Arabia, Morocco and Libya) will be over 1.5 billion. Countries such as Russia and Germany have shrinking populations. By 2050 the Yemen will have a bigger population than Germany; Iran will have a bigger population that Russia. If any of these countries obtain nuclear weapons, the world political situation will be very dangerous indeed.

But none of these demographic changes compare in scale with China, where in the past twenty years we have witnessed the largest migration of human population in history. Since 1985 nearly 250 million Chinese have moved from the interior and the western provinces to within ninety miles of the coast. This is what is really driving the boom in China: the shift of workers to the coastal factories; the growth of a new middle class in Guangzhou, Shanghai and Beijing; and the rapid growth of exports from these new industrial regions around the Pearl and Yangtze rivers.

One striking factor is that China is ageing faster than any other country in history – it is unique in growing old before it has grown rich, because of the one-child policy introduced in 1980. By 2025 the working-age population will start shrinking. By contrast, India will probably be the fastest-growing economy among the big four (as Goldman Sachs called Brazil, Russia, India and China in the *BRIC Report*), because it is a younger country with a faster-growing population. However, it does not have the same resources devoted to education as China, and there is a much higher rate of illiteracy. China will invest heavily in education and this will be the key to its continued economic success.

One worry is that in both China and India there is a heavily skewed sex ratio in favour of boys. In China there are 118 boys to every 100 girls, compared with the natural ratio of 105. In some of the more prosperous states of India, such as Delhi, where pre-natal scans have become readily available, the ratio at birth is 122 boys to 100 girls. Nobody knows what the results of this rather unique human intervention in biology will be. Some believe that it will increase the likelihood of war or social disruption.

It is estimated that on current trends the population of China may stabilize at 1.5 billion by the year 2050. No country in the world has ever had to cope with the problems of economic development for such a large number of people. As yet the problems of this vast population have scarcely affected the rest of the world but it is not hard to imagine that an economic or political convulsion among the more educated members of the population, in the search for new freedoms, could produce a large number of new refugees. In the past 150 years, the Taiping rebellion, the Sino-Japanese war and the Communist takeover in 1949 all had this consequence. As recently as 1962 a bad harvest and starvation in many parts of southern China brought more than 100,000 people into Hong Kong.

EDUCATION

The East–West Pendulum argues that China (and probably India too) is only regaining the position in world trade and global GDP that it used to have one or two centuries ago. However, it is not just population, but education, which is the key to Asia's success. If demographics alone was the explanation for economic growth then Africa would

Table 5.6: Education and science

- **325,000 new engineers graduate annually in China**

- **INTEL's High School Science Fair**

- **Research and development in technology**

- **Biotechnology in Shanghai**

today be a major destination for foreign investors. Human capital, as founding father Lee Kan Yew constantly reminded his fellow citizens in Singapore, is the real key to success and growth. Anyone who has lived in Hong Kong, Singapore or Taiwan can attest to the tremendous thirst for knowledge and self-improvement that characterizes the younger Chinese generation. Obviously the greater freedom to trade with the outside world and become an entrepreneur (or, as the Chinese call it, 'plunge into the bitter sea' of capitalism) is a vital factor, but the root explanation for China's growing boom in trade compared to past centuries is education. The internet has also contributed to China's rapid catch-up because of the spread of knowledge and ideas.

PROBLEMS FOR CHINA

The internal problems and challenges facing China, all observers agree, include the widening gap between rich and poor and between the coast and the interior provinces. (Although, as Professor Chen comments, this is not as bad as it sounds, because of the large amount of money remitted from the economic migrants in the coastal factories back to their home villages, where many new homes are being built.) The social problems faced by China today include the destruction of the traditional family because of this vast population migration and also because of the ageing population. In ten years' time, in 2015, about 25% of the Chinese population, which will then be around 1.4 billion, will be over sixty-five years old. Japan and European countries are experiencing the same demographic shift to older populations, but they usually have large pensions and savings schemes. There is little or no welfare net in China and the old people will be dependent on their families. The one-child policy, which has been in effect since 1970, means that there is a narrowing of the demographic pyramid at the base: fewer and fewer children, mostly boys, and it has been called, 'a society with no uncles or aunties'. Nevertheless, the Chinese family tradition, and Confucian respect for parents, and for the aged, continues to be very strong.

The environment is certainly one of China's greatest challenges, as it rapidly industrializes and automobile ownership grows. In some regions, for example the Pearl River estuary, and around Hong Kong, the water is badly polluted, and also the air quality is low in many cities, especially large inland cities like Chongqing.

With the approach of the Olympic Games in 2008, Beijing is a shining example of what can be done with government support and pollution controls. All coal fires were stopped in 2000, just as they had been in London in 1954 after the 'smog', and the air quality has notably improved. Every year about a million trees are planted in and around Beijing to prevent the dust storms coming in from Mongolia and the Gobi desert. Emission controls are also strict on trucks and cars in the capital, though not throughout the country. Water shortages are becoming more serious with the diminishing acreage of agricultural land.

Even between different Chinese provinces there is local protectionism. For example, Shanghai traffic is dominated by Volkswagens, whereas in the south Citroens and Hondas predominate. Different brands of beer are sold in different parts of the country. There are tariffs prevailing on trucking routes between different regions. Local municipalities support their own home-grown products. Bureaucracy and red tape is still a major brake on business.

Among other major problems that China could face in the next twenty years are:

Political instability;
The banking system;
Piracy and copyright infringement;
Corruption.

RISKS

In trying to make intelligent forecasts for Asia and think of the risks which investors should consider, I outlined in the first edition of *The East–West Pendulum* the possible catastrophes, either environmental, economic or political, that could affect investment in this area of the world. Among these I listed the following:

1. A major earthquake in Tokyo (which would impact world financial markets).
2. The volcanoes and earthquakes around the Pacific Rim – the tsunami on 26 December 2004 reminded us of the terrific damage to life that such an event can cause, although the economic impact in Indonesia, Sri Lanka and Thailand was limited.
3. Environmental risk and the decline of the water supply in China for example, which could cause severe drought or famine.
4. Military conflicts:
   a. North and South Korea
   b. Taiwan and China
   c. IndoChina
   d. Central Asia.

SPACE

One final key development in the next twenty years will be China's space programme. Very little news about this strategic area reaches the West. In 2004 China surprised almost everyone by putting its first man in space, while America and Russia have downgraded their space programmes because of funding difficulties. China continues to place major emphasis on the development of space exploration, of satellites, the military use of space and possible landings on the moon and other planets. In his book *2061*, the great science-fiction writer and prophet Arthur C. Clarke predicted that the Chinese, by that date, would be the global leaders in space exploration and colonization. Much will depend on the relative economic development of China and America, but it is not too fanciful to suppose that China could take the lead in this area within fifty years.

FORECAST

Many of the challenges facing China in the years to 2020 are challenges that are equally pertinent to other regions of the world. The challenge that rapid industrial growth poses for the environment and health is one that affects every developing nation, but is more acute in China with its large and concentrated population and its lack of clean water supplies. How China tackles the water shortage and the pollution of its rivers and air will be of great importance to the rest of the world. In this sense too the Beijing Olympic Games in 2008 will be a symbolic showpiece of Chinese achievement and modernization.

Another aspect of Chinese rapid economic growth is the growing disparity of incomes, which is also something that we can observe in Russia, India, Brazil and every developing nation. Nowhere has it evolved more rapidly than in China. Under the rule of Mao Zedong (from 1949 to 1976), China was the most egalitarian nation on earth, where everybody wore the same clothes and rode the same kind of bicycle. Thirty years later China has both billionaires and dirt-poor peasants. The new Chinese government under President Hu Jintao and Prime Minister Wen Jiabao is very conscious of this widening gap and has tried to address it through directing investment to the poorer interior provinces, but it may be said that China, like the United States, is a land of opportunity and not, like some nations in Europe, a land of envy. Every young Chinese sees the opportunity to migrate to Shanghai and make his or her fortune in the new growth economy.

In conclusion, China's greatest challenge is how to maintain stability while continuing to provide its people as a whole with better living standards. The confidence of China's people and its leaders today cannot be underestimated. The danger is that this becomes arrogance or national pride taken to an extreme degree, which might adversely affect relations with China's neighbours and international partners. The fact that China's leaders are very sensitive to and aware of this danger bodes well for China peacefully taking its place again in the cabinet of nations as a leading global power and benevolent influence on the global economy and in global politics.

Investment Conclusions

1. **The East and West** are more interdependent than ever before, both in their economic relations, trade and investment and also in the increasingly close correlation of capital markets' performance.

2. **China's economy** is increasingly sensitive to the US economy and to the vagaries of the US consumer. Foreign trade represents just under 50% of China's GNP (Walmart alone buys about 5% of China's exports). The long boom in US consumer spending will, in the normal way of the business cycle, reach a downturn of 1–2 years quite soon, and there could be significant impact on the manufacturing sector that dominates China's coastal provinces, on employment and on the social stability of the eastern part of China.

Table 6.1: The three economic blocs in 2020

	East Asia	Europe	North America
GDP			
2004 USD bn	8,959	14,142	13,406
2020 (Forecast) USD bn	25,977	29,383	32,300*
GDP per capita 2004 USD	2,761	19,479	31,177
Average annual real GDP growth (1994–2003)	3.80	2.10	3.20
Population (mn)			
2004	3,245	726	430
2020	3,768	671	500

*Based on Credit Suisse First Boston research. Figure is different to the estimated figure from *The Economist*

Table 6.2: New Chinese multinationals

- Lenovo / IBM
- TCL / Thomson
- HAIER / MAYTAG
- CNOOC / Unocal

3. For **Japan**, foreign trade represents only 18.8% of GNP. Nevertheless, within Japan's foreign-trade sector, China represents 10% of exports and nearly 20% of imports, having overtaken the USA. The US and China are the twin locomotives of Japan's export sector.

    This is even more true of **South Korea** (China is 15% of exports), of **Taiwan** (24% via Hong Kong), and of the South-East Asian countries. For all the Asian nations, China is the new trading partner with the fastest growth and greatest potential.

4. **Free trade within Asia** will be a growing trend over the next fifteen years, leading to a boom in manufactured exports to China and commodity exports from Australia, Indonesia, Malaysia, Thailand and the smaller Asian nations. Technology too will be a key sector with parts and components assembled in different Asian locations for export to developed markets. Hong Kong and Taiwan have led the way in the trend towards '**platform companies**' with design-technological knowhow, marketing and management in one location and chief assembly manufacturing in another location, usually mainland China.

5. **Travel and tourism** will be a key growth sector of the next twenty years, with an expected 100 million Chinese tourists travelling overseas every year; their main destinations will be Hong Kong, Thailand, Malaysia, Australia and then the USA and Europe. **Hotels and airlines** in the Asian countries will be major beneficiaries (Singapore Airlines, Cathay Pacific, Malaysian, Thai and Chinese Airlines). Among hotel groups, Shangri-la, Mandarin Oriental and major Western chains: Marriott, Hilton, Four Seasons.

    Hong Kong Disneyland will open in September 2005 and is expected to attract over 10 million Chinese visitors annually. Judging from the fact that Macau's monthly turnover in gambling is now greater than Las Vegas, with nearly 2 million mainland Chinese visitors a month, the shares of **Walt Disney** may do very well in the next two years.

6. **Property** in Hong Kong and Singapore will benefit from the wave of Chinese overseas investment.

7. **Art and antiques** will also be a destination for new Chinese wealth. Unlike the Japanese in the 1980s buying French Impressionist paintings, the Chinese will be buying back their own heritage and art treasures. The Sung and Tang dynasties have lagged behind the rise in prices of the Ming and Ching dynasties' ceramics and may catch up. The greatest appreciation will probably come in **modern Chinese art**, painting done since the 1949 liberation.

8. **Education** is the greatest hunger among young Chinese as can also be observed in Hong Kong and Taiwan: there will be an unprecedented demand for places at major Western universities such as Harvard, Yale, Princeton, Stanford, Oxford, Cambridge and others. The teaching of English in China will become a major growth industry, as well as management courses by Western consultants.

9. **A wave of innovation** will characterize the next fifteen years in information technology, biotechnology, nanotechnology and healthcare and medicine. One of the accelerating factors for this knowledge boom will be the internet and the access of young Chinese graduate engineers and scientists to the latest Western patents and inventions. Nevertheless, I firmly predict that the world will be surprised by the wave of Chinese inventions and new medical ideas which will benefit Western patients during the next twenty years. Investment in the Shanghai-based **biotechnology** industry could be the most profitable placement in 2005–25.

10. **The environment** will be the major problem and crisis of the next twenty years as the 2.5 billion people of China and India aspire to a middle-class living standard with dramatic growth not only in industrial production and factory emissions, but also in the demand for automobiles, motorbikes, housing, refrigerators, air conditioning and other contributors to global warming. The rise in global warming between 1985 and 2005 must be largely attributed to the industrialization of China, which has far fewer environmental constraints and regulations than the USA and Western Europe. This trend will accelerate in the next twenty years. The crisis will be felt globally, but nowhere more acutely than in China itself, with polluted air, water and health hazards from industrial waste. Technology will have to solve the problems created by this environmental crisis and there will be opportunities to invest in companies providing clean water and clean air. The Beijing Olympic Games in 2008 will be a major factor in putting China on the spot to improve environmental standards.

The environmental and health crisis in China may well produce (as Chernobyl in 1986 accelerated the demise of Communism) a **social and political crisis** leading to a change in the status of the Chinese Communist Party. The most likely outcome would be a peaceful evolution towards a one-party state such as Japan

(Liberal Democratic Party) and Singapore (People's Action Party), where a social-democrat party in China provides the stability and continuity which most of the population desire, but going through the forms of democracy and responding to the vocal needs of an increasingly affluent middle class. Another parallel can be drawn with Taiwan in the 1985–2005 period, evolving from an authoritarian rule by the Kuomintang towards a multi-party democracy.

11. Such a political evolution within China would have major consequences for **China's foreign policy** and foreign relations, for Tibet, for Taiwan, for Hong Kong and perhaps for the support that the Chinese government currently gives to the ruling military clique in Myanmar (Burma). A Chinese ruling party which was more responsive to democratic demands might have to modify its human-rights policy.

12. **Major conflicts** within Asia in the next twenty years which might disrupt economic growth would be China and Taiwan, North and South Korea, China and Japan, and discontent among the Muslim populations of Indonesia, Malaysia, and the Philippines. The last twenty years suggest that economic growth and pragmatism will take precedence over military adventurism. A peaceful federal solution encompassing China, Taiwan, Hong Kong and Macau would lead to unprecedented economic growth and a boom in trade and investment. Investors might consider that Taipei becomes a major play on China if the threat of conflict is removed, as the Hong Kong stock market has been for the last ten years.

13. Despite the unprecedented speed and size of the boom in China's economy, the **business cycle** has not been abolished and the laws of supply and demand still prevail. The over-investment and oversupply in certain manufacturing sectors will lead to a fall in prices and a collapse in profits. Toys, textiles and shoes

were the early victims of this oversupply in low-tech, low-labour-cost products. The **automobile industry** in China is also going to suffer from a collapse in profits from the over-investment by General Motors, Ford, Volkswagen, Honda, Toyota, Nissan, Peugeot and Renault. The value of **Shanghai apartments** will also fall as a result of overbuilding. The mobile-phone business in China is beginning to suffer from oversupply and falling prices. This is the major difficulty for investors wishing to participate in the Chinese boom; profits continually disappoint. The 'A' Share markets in Shanghai and Shenzhen have been the worst performing in the world in 2000–5. Oversupply of shares of state-owned enterprises is the major cause behind the disillusionment and anger of domestic Chinese investors today.

14. **Currencies:** The Asian countries' trade and current-account surplus and accumulated savings is the counter-balancing factor to the enormous US national debt and growing annual trade deficit and the chronic deficit within the European Union. This will result in a continued decline in the US dollar and probable weakness in the Euro, strengthening Japanese yen and Chinese renminbi as well as other Asian currencies, for instance the Singapore dollar. Like Japan after the Plaza accord of 1985, a strong yen produced visible Japanese wealth and high real-estate prices. Asian wealth will become more visible as the currency realignment continues in the next 5–10 years. **Commodity currencies** such as the Australian dollar, South African rand and oil-based currencies (such as the Russian rouble) will continue to be strong.

15. **Commodity prices** will closely follow the trend of the Chinese economy. This has been true of copper and oil in the past five years and the trend will be maintained. We are probably in a 10–15-year bull market for commodities, not only industrial metals, but also gold and silver; not only oil and gas, but also food products such as sugar, wheat, cotton, wool, soy beans and coffee. Every product of which the middle class of China (and India)

demands more will rise in price unless supply can be quickly increased.

16. **Chinese overseas investment** will be a key trend in the mergers-and-acquisitions business of international investment banks. The recent purchase for US$1.7 billion of the IBM personal-computer division by the Chinese computer maker Lenovo is the first sign. The CNOOC attempt to buy Unocal is another early warning that China's thirst for energy will lead it to acquisitions of major Western oil companies with significant energy reserves in stable locations, especially in Asia. **Natural-gas** companies could be an especially attractive target.

17. The best **long-term investment** in Asia will be in well managed, financially sound, dividend-paying companies listed on well regulated exchanges with a good legal system and transparency and fair treatment of minority shareholders. The **indirect** route to investing in China (i.e. what China needs from overseas) may well outperform direct investment.

THE CHINESE RENMINBI REVALUATION

The July 2005 decision to revalue the RMB against the dollar was not only a Chinese response to US pressure, in the face of the rising trade deficit with China. The US Congress passed a bill in April 2005, with an overwhelming majority, threatening China with protectionist measures if it did not revalue. China has reacted cautiously and undertaken an initial small adjustment of the currency, but it may be expected, over time, to result in a more significant revaluation.

This may be a trigger for a wide range of revaluations against the US dollar in Asia. The Singapore dollar and the Korean won have already appreciated by 15%. The Thai baht, Malaysian ringgit, Indonesian rupiah and Indian rupee may all follow. The new Taiwanese dollar is likely to follow the renminbi.

Total Asian Foreign Exchange Reserves amount to more than US$2.3 trillion and enormous purchasing power is represented by these Asian savings which are now truly reflected in the strength of currency, enabling Asians to buy Western goods and products at better prices.

These are some parallels in history:

- The 1949 devaluation of the pound sterling against the US dollar led to a wave of US spending in Europe.

- The 1985 Plaza accord – the Japanese yen moved from 250 yen to the dollar, quite rapidly, to 120 yen. In 1985–7 this led to a boom in US shares and also a rise in real-estate values in Japan. At the peak of the Japanese boom in 1989 the Nikkei was at 40,000 and the Emperor's Palace grounds in central Tokyo were valued at slightly more than the State of California.

Whilst not predicting that a Chinese renminbi revaluation would produce the dramatic results that the Plaza accord did, nevertheless it is an important historical change, which will lead to the new Chinese wealth being more truly reflected in world markets (either in real estate or in securities).

Other possible consequences include renewed strength in demand for resources sought by China – iron ore, copper, oil and gas and various soft commodities; and a possible boom in Hong Kong assets if the Hong Kong dollar maintains its peg to the US dollar.

Companies with renminbi costs will suffer, whereas those that have sales or earnings in China, and are importing raw materials from overseas will gain and profit. One certain result of this important currency realignment is the beginning of a new trend of Asian financial strength and influence that will last for the next 5–10 years.

Postscript

Two recently published books on China provide a sobering contrast to the naïve optimism of many Western observers. As one seasoned Sinophile puts it: 'China is like a large lake, in which we all see what we want to see', in other words our own vision of China, 'but none of us can see the bottom of the lake'. Jung Chang and John Holliday's masterful new biography of *Mao* reminds us that the legacy of this monstrous dictator, whose autocratic rule of China from 1949 to 1976 cost 70 million lives, is still alive in China today. His portrait still hangs prominently over Tiananmen Square, and no repudiation of the Maoist legacy is likely or possible under the present rule of the Communist Party, despite the fact that the Chinese economy, with its new, open, global and capitalist character today, has effectively repudiated the ideas of Marx and Mao almost entirely.

Another book, *Wild West China*, draws our attention to the Uighurs in Xinjiang and the Han Chinese immigration, which has in recent decades overwhelmed the western province. There too, the legacy of Mao persists in the network of Gulag prison camps which are strung around the western borders of China and still contain hundreds of thousands of political prisoners.

No amount of starry-eyed optimism about the economic prospects for investment and business in China should blind us to the fact that it is still a totalitarian police state. The insecurity of many of China's new capitalists, and their desire to park their newly won wealth in safe offshore locations, may stem from this invisible background, and also from the universal folk memory of the Cultural Revolution, which has the effect that all Chinese, particularly those aged between forty and sixty, fear, above all, a return to the chaos, anarchy, and violence of that lost decade between 1966 and 1976, when many lost not only their years of education, but even their families. Because of this terrible experience, many in China today justify the crackdown at

Tiananmen Square in June 1989 as a safer alternative than to allow the student uprising to develop into another cultural revolution, unlikely as it may seem to Westerners.

All of this background is important to us as investors in considering the political risks and the difficulty of making any intelligent forecast about where China may be in ten or fifteen years' time politically and economically. Chinese history teaches us to expect constant surprises and unexpected shocks, which upset the smooth upward charts of the planners, developers and stockbrokers.

Appendix: GDP table

2004	Population (m)	Nominal GDP (USD bn)	Nominal GDP PPP (USD bn)	GDP per capita (USD)	GDP per capita (USD) at PPP
US	293.0	11,735	11,735	40,050	40,050
Singapore	4.2	107	131	25,290	31,100
Hong Kong	7.0	165	211	23,600	30,310
Australia	20.1	617	602	30,650	29,940
Japan	127.3	4,666	3,708	36,646	29,119
Taiwan	22.5	305	600	13,548	26,610
South Korea	48.2	681	1,065	14,120	22,090
Malaysia	25.5	118	269	4,620	10,570
Thailand	64.5	164	512	2,530	7,930
China	1,299.8	1,594	7,547	1,230	5,810
Philippines	86.2	86	383	1,000	4,440
Indonesia	223.8	258	828	1,150	3,700
Sri Lanka	19.3	20	69	1,030	3,570
India	1,080.3	658	3,290	609	3,050
Vietnam	82.6	45	224	545	2,720
Pakistan	153.7	95	342	617	2,230
Laos	5.8	2	11	376	1,940
Bangladesh	149.8	57	237	379	1,580
Cambodia	14.5	5	23	331	1,580
Myanmar	50.2	9	38	186	749

Source: The Economist